To Peter
Thanks for your support
Richard Muth

Here are excerpts from this rousing work by an elected official known for his candor—candor *while in office* and not after the fires of political ambition have grown cold.

"Until we hold politicians accountable for their cowardly and shameless appeals to our baser instincts, until we acquire the purpose not only to admire political courage and integrity, but also to raise up those who display such qualities, we will get the kind of government we deserve."

"Let me start with the hard, honest truth about property taxes. Your property taxes will go up every year because the cost of running this town goes up every year, and with very little land remaining for development, we can no longer rely on an expanding tax base to cover the increased costs of doing business. Nor can we count on higher state aid; the state's finances are on life support . . . . To survive this economic 'perfect storm,' we must continue eliminating waste and managing the municipal budget wisely."

"A community is more than just a means to fulfill basic governmental services, like police and fire protection, road repair and garbage pick-up. It is more than zoning ordinances, rules and regulations. A community must also have a soul, a spirit that gives voice to everything that is creative, inspirational and divine in the human condition."

"Just once, I'd like us to elect a president who has read a history book, and I don't mean the Action Comic Book version. Far too often, our presidents have ignored the lessons of history, dooming thousands of young men, mostly, but now more and more women, to pay the price for their ignorance."

"I have a few ideas about reducing the cost of municipal government, to stave off the inevitable day when taxes must be increased. For example, we must take what will surely be an unpopular stand with our borough employees. We must learn how to say no to them, and it pains me greatly to have to do that. For the most part, they are wonderful, hardworking people, who have their own problems trying to raise families and make ends meet. But we can't keep agreeing to salary increases far in excess of annual cost of living adjustments, or to free medical insurance for the entire family."

"When seniors on fixed incomes are forced to sell homes they've lived in 40 or 50 years and raised their children in, when they must leave family, friends, doctors and other close relationships behind because they can no longer afford property taxes, when they're banished to so-called 'adult-living' communities in Toms River, or points farther south, our town will become the poorer for it. I cherish having these old-timers around, listening to their stories, and having their dignity and character serve as guideposts for young people. God forbid we become a homogenized community of thirty-something or forty-something upwardly mobile couples with 2.3 kids."

"We will be faced with great challenges this year, not the least of which is the budget and its effect on property taxes.
How we meet those challenges is yet to be determined, but I have every hope it will be with leadership, political courage and wisdom."

"Every once in a while, I observe someone who epitomizes the lawyer as hero. Not an Atticus Finch, or a product of Grisham's or Turow's creative talent, but a real-life lawyer, slugging it out for a principle, no matter how reprehensible the client or unpopular the cause."

"Dear friends and fellow citizens, I must tell you I was disheartened by the poor attendance at this year's Veterans' Day ceremony. At the end of the short program, I couldn't help but reflect that, of almost 15,000 residents, less than 20 found the time to attend. I know we all honor these men and women who fought so bravely in by-gone wars and who are fighting and dying now in a raging war with no end in sight. Please, in future, let us demonstrate—for them and their families, before these old-timers are gone—the honor and respect we all feel in our hearts. Let us stand with them on their special days of remembrance, as they stood up for us when our democracy was in peril."

"Tony Soprano and his crew have put New Jersey on the map, but in a way that perpetuates an unfortunate stereotype. There is a different kind of Italian-American family saga that needs to be told, the one I experienced growing up in New Jersey in the 1940's and '50's. It was less exciting—everybody worked, nobody got 'whacked'—but more representative of nearly two million New Jersey residents who proudly proclaim their Italian ancestry."

"Undoubtedly, I shall incur the wrath of teachers, police, and other government employees because of my stand on what they consider to be entitlements. But I do not despair over the possibility of being a one-term mayor. Don't get me wrong—I love this job. Even so, I won't get down from my bully pulpit to keep it."

"I began my term as mayor fairly brimming with ideas and ideals, but perhaps a bit too cocksure for my own good. Yes, I had been elected with 62% of the vote in a huge turnout. But I soon learned that criticism comes easy; it is much more difficult to govern. The hard part was about to begin."

PASSION, POLITICS AND PATRIOTISM

IN SMALL-TOWN AMERICA

Confessions of a plain-talking,
independent Mayor

Richard Muti

WingSpan Press

Printed in the United States of America

Published by WingSpan Press, Livermore, CA
www.wingspanpress.com

The WingSpan name, logo and colophon are the trademarks of WingSpan Publishing.

Front cover photograph: Christopher Ottaunick
Back cover photograph: S. Stava

ISBN 978-1-59594-225-8
First edition 2008

Library of Congress Control Number 2007935747

Contents

IT IS NOT the critic who counts; not the man who points out how the strong man stumbles, or where the doer of deeds could have done them better. The credit belongs to the man who is actually in the arena, whose face is marred by dust and sweat and blood; who strives valiantly; who errs, who comes short again and again, because there is no effort without error and shortcoming; but who does actually strive to do the deeds; who knows great enthusiasms, the great devotions; who spends himself in a worthy cause; who at the best knows in the end the triumph of high achievement, and who at the worst, if he fails, at least fails while daring greatly. . . .

Theodore Roosevelt

Preface

On November 5, 2002, the people of Ramsey (pop. 14,500) in Bergen County, New Jersey, elected me, a 62-year old political novice, as their mayor.

It was a homecoming for me. I was born and raised in Ramsey, attended its public schools and played Little League ball on its fields. Indeed, my immigrant grandparents, Sergio and Rosaria Muti, had settled in Ramsey in 1911, one of the few Italian families in town at that time. Now, almost 100 years later, a quarter of the population has some Italian blood.

My father, Mauro Richard Muti, was a lifelong resident of Ramsey, until his death at age 87. In 1939, he married my mother, Mafalda Milano, a 19-year old beauty from neighboring Waldwick, and, together, they opened the Community Lunch, a fixture on Main Street for 25 years and gathering place for townsfolk active in community life—business, politics, and government.

U.S. Congressman Bill Widnall bowled on the Community Lunch team when he was home from Washington. My father served as president of the Chamber of Commerce. He was a Ramsey fireman—one of his proudest activities—and was president of the Republican Club. In the mid-1950s, he was elected to the Borough Council, the first Italian-American in Ramsey's history to win a seat on the governing body. He was reelected twice and served nine years, five as council president. All this, while working 70-80 hours a week in his luncheonette. My father left the council in the mid-1960s when he was elected tax assessor, a post he would hold until his 81st year. He stepped down only after suffering a heart attack, which began his slow but steady decline in health.

I started working in the Community Lunch, after school and

on Saturdays, in the fourth or fifth grade and remember my father tying a folded white apron on me so it wouldn't drag as I waited on customers and washed dishes (by hand—*pearl diving* my father called it). Eventually, I worked my way up to the grill and steam table as a pint-sized but aptly named "short-order" cook. One of the most thrilling moments, and scariest, was the first time my father ran off to fight a fire (he drove a fire truck garaged down the street from the restaurant behind Micek's Bakery) and left me, a grade-schooler, in charge of the place.

I was an observant boy—a reader and a listener. My time in the Community Lunch was spent not just diving for pearls, but also listening to pearls, of wisdom—adult discussions about politics and government at every level. Like, *Who would succeed Soviet dictator Josef Stalin*? Not an inconsequential issue in those Cold War days of frequent hydrogen bomb tests and brinkmanship diplomacy. Stalin had died suddenly, and the Communist Party's determination of his successor might have meant the difference between the status quo, however stressful, and nuclear annihilation. I remember poring over *New York Daily News* photos of the five or six men thought most likely to replace Stalin and settling on my choice, a kindly looking man named Beria. Alas, Beria was "liquidated" within weeks. I later learned he was the murderous head of the KGB.

Or, *was President Truman right in firing General Douglas MacArthur*? Civilian control over the military—pretty heady Constitutional stuff for an 11-year old to be pondering. I came down on President Truman's side.

Or, *should millionaire Malcolm Forbes be the next governor of New Jersey*? When Forbes, a maverick Republican, lost the 1953 gubernatorial primary to a dubious party hack, my father, "Mr. Republican" in the Borough of Ramsey, had no qualms about supporting Robert Meyner, the Democratic nominee and eventual winner of the election.

I suppose it was preordained that I would enter politics myself one day, albeit late in life. After graduating from Ramsey High School and spending two years at civilian colleges, I entered the United States Naval Academy at Annapolis, graduating in 1964, marrying a few weeks later, and entering flight training that same year. My first solo landing on an aircraft carrier—in a T-28 Trojan, which looked and felt like a WWII fighter plane—was *and still is* the most exciting moment of my life. I served five years as a Naval Aviator, flying patrol bombers, and left the service when my tour of duty ended to accept a scholarship to Harvard Business School.

After getting my MBA degree in 1971, I worked in the real estate industry, first in the Midwest, then in Pennsylvania and New York—successful but never making a mark in business. I'm one of the least wealthy members of my Harvard Business School class, if what I read in the alumni magazine is true.

By this time, I had settled with my wife and three children in Sparta, New Jersey, about an hour from Ramsey. I saw my parents at least twice a week, not just to check on their welfare as they grew older, but because I wanted to spend time with them. My mother's cooking was an added incentive. (*"Richard, are you coming over tonight? I made pasta 'cheech'."* Or, *"Richard, I made ravioli. You better come before your cousin Frank eats them all."* Invariably, I would answer, *"Yeah, Ma, I'll be there."*)

Discontented with my business career, I decided to study law and entered the Rutgers Law School night program in 1976. It was a grind—commuting to school in Newark four nights a week while working full time. But I stuck to it and became a lawyer in 1980 at age 40. Then, I left a real estate job paying $80,000—big money in those days—to accept an $18,000 position as an assistant prosecutor in the Bergen County Prosecutor's Office. You can see why I'm not rich.

I found my niche as a trial prosecutor. Over a prosecutorial career spanning 19 years, both part-time at the municipal level in Sparta and full-time at the county level in Bergen County, I presented hundreds of cases to grand juries, prosecuted 2,000 drunk drivers, and served as lead prosecutor in more than 40 jury trials involving major crimes like armed robbery, arson, kidnapping, and murder.

Thorough preparation was the key to my success in trying cases. Before cross-examining a key witness—a doctor or other professional, for example—I would study everything that witness had ever written. Once, in a murder case, I read a quote to a psychiatrist who was trying to persuade the jury that the defendant was insane. The quote completely contradicted the doctor's testimony on the witness stand. He denigrated the quoted passage, saying that the author was, at best, mistaken and, at worst, incompetent. The case was won for the State when I produced the medical journal article in which the quote appeared, revealing the author to be the witness, himself. It was my "Perry Mason" moment.

I tried the first case in New Jersey in which hypnosis was allowed to refresh a witness's memory. In doing so, I became something of an expert on hypnosis. I tried the first death-eligible murder case in Bergen County after the state legislature reinstated the death penalty in the early 1980s. It involved a hooker who killed her john when, she claimed, he got rough with her. She pulled a knife in self-defense, and he ran into it. Six times. Because of extenuating circumstances, I decided, with the concurrence of my boss, not to seek the death penalty.

I loved standing before a jury, having all the facts and organization of a complex case in my head, and arguing for the cause of truth and justice. Corny, I know, but that's the way I felt. I think jurors genuinely liked a prosecutor they perceived to be fair but tough. My overall conviction rate was 99%.

That dream career came to an abrupt end when I was fired by the Bergen County Prosecutor in 2000. In addition to my trial duties, I was also the office's chief administrator, handling financial and personnel matters. I objected, privately, to several actions that I thought my boss was taking inappropriately. He was the type who didn't like subordinates voicing opinions that differed from his, and I was certainly not the "yes man" type. Finally, when he was about to spend $7,000,000 in public money for what I thought was a wasteful project and had counseled against, I brought my misgivings to County officials. I was fired that same day, just ten months shy of qualifying for full retirement benefits. A dumb career move, perhaps, but something I had to do.

The year 2000 was not a good year for me. Like most people, I had ups and downs throughout my life—a divorce in the early 1990s, remarriage a few years later (yes, "Love *is* wonderful the second time around"), and loss of family members—but nothing to compare with 2000. My father died in March, a year after one of my sisters died. Dad's final six months were filled with suffering. If you've read this far, I think you understand what he meant to me. In June, my sister-in-law, whom I was very close to, died suddenly.

My mother-in-law had a heart attack at her daughter's wake and died. In August, I got fired. To borrow Queen Elizabeth's phrase, it was my *annus horribilis*.

Imbued with the work ethic of my parents and grandparents, I had labored all my life with a joy usually reserved for recreational pursuits. I loved to work, perhaps to my detriment for it often caused me to neglect family responsibilities, a factor in my divorce. Suddenly, at age 60, I found myself on the street looking for a job. I was devastated, both emotionally and, because of the low priority I had always attached to money-making, financially.

Despite hundreds of inquiries made and resumes distributed, despite what I thought were impressive credentials (Naval Academy, military officer, Harvard MBA, Rutgers Law degree), and despite a lifetime of nose-to-the-grindstone work habits in leadership roles, I couldn't find a job. When asked in interviews my reason for leaving the Prosecutor's Office, I responded truthfully. I had been fired for a noble cause—a protest against wasting public money—but no one wanted to hire a 60-year old who had just been fired, whatever the reason.

Finally, there came a time when I had to do something I dreaded, something that was more humiliating than I could imagine. I went on unemployment. I had paid into the unemployment fund my entire life and, in a way, it was some of my own money I would be getting back. Nevertheless, as I stood in line to collect benefits and answered questions to show I really was trying to find work, I felt like a worthless bum on the public dole.

Eventually, I landed part-time jobs at three universities— William Paterson, Fairleigh Dickinson, and Rutgers—teaching freshman English, criminal justice, and American government and politics. The pay was terrible for the amount of work involved. One of the dirty secrets of higher education is the paltry sums and zero benefits colleges pay their "adjunct" professors, who make up 50% of the faculty at most public institutions. But I enjoyed teaching, and those jobs helped me to survive financially until I qualified for a New Jersey pension, based on 25 years of public service, in July 2002. I continued teaching thereafter, even though finances were no longer a problem. I had to work; I had to be productive. It was my nature. So I kept at it, grading papers, reading student essays, and planning lessons that I hoped would instill in my students the same love of government and politics and writing and justice that I had felt all those years.

Then, something happened.

After my father died and after I was fired, I moved back home to Ramsey, a return to my roots, so to speak. Ramsey was part of my healing process in 2000: walking the streets and fields I had walked and played in as a child; seeing the old Community Lunch storefront in its latest incarnation as a specialty chocolate shop and, later, a mortgage brokerage office; greeting people—old-timers who had known me and my family from the early days and who had not yet been forced out of town by rising property taxes. I felt young again.

Once home, I renewed my interest in local politics . . . and didn't like what I saw. The mayor and council had lost touch with the people, it seemed. I have always been a proponent of term limits for all elected officials. Ramsey had a mayor who had been in office for sixteen years and who was getting ready to run for another term. He was a Republican, as were all six councilmen.

Ramsey had been a Republican stronghold forever, even when I was a kid, with only brief interludes of one or two Democrats holding office. Political power of that sort breeds arrogance and stagnation, no matter how good-intentioned or honest the people in office may be. For the prior eight years, Democrats hadn't even bothered to field candidates in any municipal elections—that's how ineffectual they had been. The last Democratic mayor had been first elected 28 years before, when my father, ever the independent thinker, had thrown his support behind the man, who then won the election by 10 votes.

Party affiliation has never meant much to me. I've been a Republican, a Democrat, and an Independent. Like my father, I vote for individuals and not their party affiliation. I voted for Barry Goldwater in 1964. Eight years later, after the debacle in Viet Nam became apparent, I harkened to WWII hero George McGovern's call to "Come home, America." I'm hard to pin a political label on—I'll take honesty over ideology every time.

My first run for political office in Ramsey actually occurred the year before I was elected mayor. In the fall of 2001, right after the events of September 11th, I resolved to do something about the state of affairs in my hometown. Three council seats were up for election that November, but it was too late to get on the ballot. So, I ran as a write-in candidate. A week before Election Day, I mailed a 3-page letter to every voter in town, explaining why I thought we needed change and asking them to write in my name— a complicated process for even the most astute voter. That was the extent of my campaign.

To everyone's astonishment, including my own, I got 600 write-in votes for councilman. It wasn't enough to win, of course, but it put me on the political map and set the stage for my landslide victory in the mayor's race one year later.

Running as a Democrat, I defeated the four-term Republican incumbent with 62% of the vote. What's more, my two council running mates, neither of whom had ever stood for office, also won their races, ousting the four-term council president in the process. Voter turnout was huge—64%, the highest in a non-presidential election for at least the last fifty years.

We won by exposing the shortcomings of one-party government and by promising to bring "Leadership for a change"—our slogan— to the people of Ramsey. I took the oath of office as mayor at 12:01 a.m. on January 1, 2003, with my wife, mother, sister, and friends looking on. It was a proud but humbling moment. I was in charge of my hometown for the next four years, responsible for the collective well being of every man, woman, and child in it.

When I moved into the mayor's office the next day, I hung two items on the wall facing my desk. A framed portrait of Harry Truman, to remind me where the buck stopped, and my father's Ramsey High School diploma, Class of 1930, to remind me who I was and what was expected of me.

Richard Muti
Ramsey, New Jersey
June 17, 2007

Chapter 1

A shorter version of this article was published as an Op-Ed piece in the Sunday, September 15, 2002, edition of The New York Times, New Jersey Section, during my campaign for mayor. I wrote it out of pride in my family and Italian-American heritage, and love for my hometown—not as a campaign tool.

THE UN-SOPRANOS

—Hard Work, Perseverance, and Nobody Gets 'Whacked'—

The "fahgeddaboudits" and "howyadoons" will spew forth like staccato bursts from a tommy gun when HBO's mob hit "The Sopranos" begins its fourth season this week. Tony Soprano and his crew have put New Jersey on the map, but in a way that perpetuates an unfortunate stereotype. There is a different kind of Italian-American family saga that needs to be told, the one I experienced growing up in the 1940's and '50's. It was less exciting—everybody worked, nobody got "whacked"—but more representative of nearly two million New Jersey residents who proudly proclaim their Italian ancestry.

I live in Ramsey, a few blocks from the gray-stuccoed house on Carol Street where my father was raised. My grandparents had nine children. That number might have increased had my grandfather not died from a work injury in 1929, just as the Great Depression was about to unfold.

My father Mauro Richard Muti, the oldest son, became head of the family at sixteen. He was able to finish high school, but continued to work after school and weekends. All four boys in the family would eventually graduate from high school. Girls, in accordance with contemporary thinking, had no need for *higher* education. They went right to work after grammar school. Aunt Jean, the youngest, was the exception. She came of age when the family's fortunes were more secure and was allowed to attend Ramsey High School.

The family survived the 1930's, thanks to the indomitable spirit of my grandmother, an illiterate peasant girl from Calabria who stood barely five feet tall. I often wonder at her accomplishment. Left destitute with nine children and no husband at the beginning of the greatest economic upheaval this country has ever known, my giant of a grandmother kept her family together, reasonably well fed and clothed. Then, just as things began to look brighter, she sent three of her sons off to war.

Uncle Vince, seriously wounded by shrapnel while serving as a B-24 tail-gunner, returned with the Purple Heart and continued his career as a letter carrier with the Ramsey Post Office. Uncle Tony, who fought with Patton's Third Army from Normandy to the Rhine, was highly decorated with medals himself, including the Bronze Star. He went to work for Curtiss-Wright building aircraft engines. Uncle Nick, a Navy man, became a bartender after his discharge. My father spent the war years on the home front organizing relief efforts and keeping watch over his mother and family, as he had done his whole life.

My parents owned the Community Lunch, a fixture on Main Street for 25 years. In the Forties, they kept it open day and night to accommodate truckers and delivery men. When both parents were working, I was dropped off at my grandmother's house on Carol Street. I loved sleeping over in my father's old bedroom, barely large enough to accommodate its single bed.

I've never been able to fall asleep quickly, even as a child, and remember lying awake listening to crickets and frogs, unaware of the romantic purpose behind their nightly serenades. And, of course, the train whistles. I liked listening to the train whistles best of all.

Ramsey was a busy railroad town in those days. Hundred-car freights lumbered through regularly. During and just after the War, we'd see artillery guns and jeeps strapped to flat cars. At times, stake-sided livestock cars were part of the mix, the protests of their hapless riders barely audible over the hypnotic clackety-clack of the rails. Freight cars fueled a boy's imagination with faraway names emblazoned on their sides— names like Norfolk and Western, Rock Island Line, Union Pacific, and, my favorite, The Route of the Phoebe Snow.

On winter mornings I could hear my grandmother in the cellar shoveling coal to stoke the furnace, which she had banked the night before. The heat would make a racket as it rose in metal ducts, and I'd wait until I felt it escaping the floor vent before leaving the warmth of my bed. As I washed up, I would smell the coffee perking in the kitchen below.

I ate the same breakfast Grandma raised her brood on— toasted day-old Italian bread, buttered and dunked in a coffee and milk mixture that nowadays would be called café latte, but which we ignorantly called half and half. As a nutritional extra, my grandmother would crack a raw egg into a cup, spoon in sugar, add a few generous dashes of red wine, and beat the concoction vigorously with a fork. The result was an eggnog like no other. I don't know what its therapeutic properties were, but I've been healthy my entire life.

I remember vendors stopping by the house on Carol Street in rickety trucks or horse-drawn wagons. Some sold fresh fish packed in ice; others sold produce. One had a knife-sharpening rig, and Grandma would periodically take her cutlery outside to have edges honed. The iceman delivered once a week, carrying in a block on his shoulder after having chiseled it to fit the ice box compartment. On hot summer days, I always got a few mouth-sized chips to cool me off.

My grandmother's kitchen was large, rectangular and usually dark. I don't think the single electric light was ever turned on in daytime—a throwback to the time when a nickel saved here and there meant the difference between having enough food and going hungry. A white porcelain table was Grandma's workstation for weekly pasta-making and all other feats of culinary magic she performed in that primitive (by today's standards) kitchen. There was no cooking smell I liked better than my grandmother's meatballs frying in a large black pan on her old-fashioned stove. After the meatballs were drained, she gently dropped them into a simmering pot of tomato sauce, but not before setting aside three or four for me. She knew I liked them best crispy and hot, right out of the frying pan.

Inspired by Grandma's cooking, I once composed a 4th grade homework paper on her kitchen table using the family's upright Remington. Assigned to write an autobiography, I cockily entitled my effort, "From Milk and Pabulum to Meatballs and Spaghetti, The Life Story of Richard Muti," foreshadowing my 60-year love affair with food.

My grandmother is gone now, of course, as is my father, Aunt Minnie, Aunt Jean and Uncle Nick. Aunt Sallie, Aunt Rosie, and Uncle Tony passed just in the last twelve months. Only Uncle Vince and Aunt Josie are left. New owners have updated the family homestead on Carol Street, hiding its stodgy gray stucco behind vinyl siding. The two pear trees I used to climb have been cut down, and the grapevine-covered arbor my grandfather built is gone, too. A lawn covers ground where my grandmother's garden once flourished. In late summer, it was filled with tomato plants heavy with fruit, squash, Swiss chard and beets. It was also my favorite spot for digging fishing worms, the big nightcrawler kind.

Now, as I lie awake at night in my own home, a few blocks from the house on Carol Street, I no longer hear crickets or frogs outside. They seem to have disappeared, as these memories of my family will disappear when I, too, am gone. Trains, although fewer, still pass through town. When sleep is difficult, their whistles have the same lulling effect on me . . . and the power to transport an aging man, back along the route of the Phoebe Snow, to his childhood in Ramsey.

Chapter 2

The issue that contributed most to my landslide victory in 2002 was the incumbent administration's outrageous compensation arrangement with the borough attorney. I uncovered this sordid state of affairs when I filed an Open Public Records request for the man's W-2 and 1099 forms and used those facts to good advantage in my campaign. After winning the race, I soon discovered the Republican majority's intention to stonewall me. They weren't about to remove the man they had kept in office for 25 years, and under our form of government, they controlled the matter. Finally, with just weeks to go before I was to be sworn in, I made this public appeal to Ramsey residents, taking out a paid ad to do so. The response was tremendous. People from both parties wrote to the newspaper and telephoned the recalcitrant Republican councilmen. Ultimately, they backed down and supported my choice for borough attorney. That one action would save taxpayers half a million dollars over my four years in office.

A Greedy Lawyer and Other Wonders of Politics

The election is over, and it is time to govern. But I need your help on something, if I am to govern effectively. You may recall that during the campaign I made an issue of the amount of money Ramsey has been paying its borough attorney. This man has been our borough attorney for more than 25 years and receives an annual salary of about $123,000, plus additional compensation at the rate of $75 per hour for every hour over 85 hours a month.

Over the past four years alone (1998-2001), we have paid the man $992,916.22 in salary and hourly fees. (It was spread out fairly evenly, so there was no spike in compensation for any extraordinary matter.) I don't have the figure yet for 2002, but have no doubt that it will be similar. On top of his monetary compensation, we have paid for his family health insurance benefits (about $12,000 per year) and social security employer taxes (about $9,000 per year). The average cost to taxpayers over the last four years has been about $270,000 per year. But there's more. We also pay for his secretarial services and provide him with a private office in the Borough Hall. When you factor all that in, we're talking about a borough attorney with an annual price tag of $300,000. That expense for a town our size is nothing short of outrageous.

There is no question that the man is a competent lawyer and that he performs many legal services for the Borough; but he also finds time to be the municipal court judge in two other municipalities and to conduct a private law practice from an office on Franklin Turnpike. So he is not devoting all his time to Ramsey. Even if he were, we do not need a full-time lawyer. If you calculate working hours based on his compensation agreement, he is spending about 50 hours a week acting as Ramsey's borough attorney, on top of his other jobs. Perhaps the man is a workhorse, but you have to question whether Ramsey is being well served by the concept of having a lawyer encamped in the Borough Hall. I couldn't find another town that does business that way. This attorney's arrangement with the Borough of Ramsey—whereby we supply him with a private office, secretarial services, all other office expenses, and family medical insurance—appears to be unique.

I compared what Ramsey is paying for legal services to what a dozen other Bergen County towns are paying. The results of that comparison confirm absolutely my contention that we are paying far too much—more than double what we should be paying. Let's look at just a few examples.

Mahwah (population 24,500) has paid its township attorney about $185,000 in 2002, year to date. This was an especially heavy litigation year for Mahwah, according to a local official. Last year, the total payment to the township attorney was about $135,000. I emphasize that these were the total payments; there were no health benefits paid, no employer social security taxes (the attorney was an independent contractor, not an employee), and no pension benefits paid. And Mahwah's attorney supplies his own office and secretarial services.

If we want to compare our experience with a town closer to Ramsey's size, we could take a look at Wyckoff (population 16,500). Wyckoff has three different attorneys performing duties that our borough attorney performs, but the total cost of those three attorneys—all specialists—is 38% of our attorney's price tag. For the first 11 months of 2002, Wyckoff paid its borough attorney $76,000. For the same period, Wyckoff paid its separate labor counsel $8,200 and its separate tax appeal counsel $20,000. The total expense for these three attorneys, extrapolated for the full 12 months of 2002, would be about $112,000. Once again, not one of these three attorneys gets health benefits or any other benefits. All of them work out of their own offices and supply their own secretarial services.

A third comparison is even more telling. Hackensack, with a population of about 45,000, is the largest municipality in Bergen County and the county seat. I spoke with the city attorney recently. He gets $7,000 a year to attend all mayor and council meetings, and he bills at $85 per hour for everything else he does. He averages $9,000 a month in billings, for a total of $115,000 per year. Hackensack has a separate tax counsel, who earns $60,000 per year, and a separate labor counsel, who earns $40,000 per year. The total for the full representation is about $215,000, and all of Hackensack's attorneys supply their own office space and secretarial services. None receives health insurance benefits.

Even with the commercial and governmental activity in Hackensack, and the fact that the population must swell to 100,000 during the workday, this busiest of Bergen County cities pays its combined legal representation about $85,000 less a year than we pay our sole borough attorney. Do you see why I am outraged?

I promised that I would try to do something about waste in our municipal government. I have found an experienced and highly competent attorney who will cost us less than $125,000 for 2003. This individual has 19 years experience as a borough attorney with another municipality in Bergen County, is a municipal court judge for three other municipalities, is a former Bergen County assistant prosecutor, and has 25 years of litigation experience. He is a 20-year resident of Ramsey, coaches youth sports, and is a parishioner at St. Paul R.C. Church; I've known him for 22 years. He contributed not one dime to my campaign. I intend to appoint him because he is a lawyer of the highest integrity, has the requisite experience, is eminently qualified for the position, and will save Ramsey taxpayers more than $150,000 a year.

But here's the problem. I can appoint the borough attorney, but the council must approve my appointment. My two running mates will support my selection of a new borough attorney, but I'm not sure about the four remaining council members. They seem satisfied with the current arrangement and don't seem willing to make a change. Unless I can get one of them to change his mind, creating a 3-3 tie and allowing me to vote to break the tie, it looks like Ramsey will be saddled with the highest paid attorney in Bergen County for at least one more year.

The four remaining council members are honorable men, and I have every hope that I can persuade one or more of them to join with my team and make this change. I have met them more than half way in many other appointments for the coming year. For example, I have advised them I will reappoint the current municipal prosecutor, who happens to be chairman of the Ramsey Republican Club, and the current public defender. I am doing so because they are both doing a good job, and I do not make appointments based on party affiliation or campaign contributions. (I don't even know what political party my prospective borough attorney belongs to—I haven't asked him.)

Sunday, January 5, 2003, is D-day. Decision day. That is the date of the governing body's annual reorganization meeting. Because I expect and hope for a good turnout, the reorganization meeting will be held in the Ramsey High School auditorium. I thank the Board of Education for their accommodation. The program begins at 1:00 p.m., but residents should arrive early to hear a stirring selection of patriotic tunes by the Ramapo Wind Symphony. The event will likely be carried over Cablevision's local access channel 72.

I need a good turnout to convince my colleagues on the council that Ramsey residents demand a change in the borough attorney situation. No, there won't be any disturbances in the audience, or vocal expressions of support. I just need as many of you as possible to sit in silent witness of the events that will unfold. The auditorium holds 900 people. We could never get that high a turnout on a Sunday afternoon in winter, with NFL playoffs and all. But if we could get 250 or 300 of you to show up in solidarity with me, I think that would be the clincher. It would get us a new borough attorney, save us $150,000, and help me immensely to do the job you elected me to do.

If you can't attend the reorganization meeting on January 5th, please send a letter right now to the Mayor and Council, Borough of Ramsey, 33 North Central Ave., Ramsey, NJ 07446, and demand that the council give their full consideration to my designation of a borough attorney. I understand their reluctance to change and, perhaps, their loyalty to the only borough attorney any of them has known during his time on the council. But if taxpayers can save $150,000 a year and still have highly competent legal representation, I contend that there is no other reasonable choice. Help me to make that point on January 5th.

You elected me by an overwhelming margin to do something about the high cost of government. Now, I need you to reinforce the message you sent on Election Day.

Chapter 3

Every New Jersey municipality starts off its year with a reorganization meeting, at which newly elected members of the governing body are sworn in and other routine business matters are carried out. People are appointed to various positions, like borough attorney, borough engineer, municipal prosecutor, zoning officer, etc. Leaders of the fire department, ambulance corps, and rescue squad are installed. Banks are named to hold public funds. In short, pretty mundane stuff, which explains why reorganization meetings are largely ignored by the public, except, of course, for family members of those being honored in some way.

Ramsey's annual meetings were usually held in the council chambers of Borough Hall. I had been officially sworn in there as mayor one minute after midnight on January 1, 2003, but was looking forward to the ceremonial trappings of my first reorganization meeting, scheduled for Sunday, January 5th.

I wanted to start off with a bang, naturally, and requested that the meeting be moved from the 130-seat capacity council chambers to the Ramsey High School auditorium, with a 900-seat capacity. I arranged for the Ramapo Wind Symphony, a regional band, to play for the event. Since this was beyond normal expectation for a meeting of this sort, I paid for the band myself. Then, I asked Ramsey residents to attend the reorganization meeting as a show of support for my administration, especially regarding the borough attorney issue. It was, perhaps, my first display of chutzpah as mayor. Egg-on-the-face time if, after moving the meeting to this larger venue and asking for support, no one showed up.

The people of Ramsey came through. I was overwhelmed by the outpouring of support. The auditorium was packed—every seat

*taken and standing-room only in the aisles and balcony. There
had to have been a thousand people there, probably ten percent of
the adult population of the town. It was the biggest audience for a
meeting of the Ramsey governing body in the town's history.*

*This is the speech I gave, extending an olive branch to my
Republican colleagues on the council.*

An Auspicious Beginning

Ladies and gentlemen, thank you for your endurance in sitting
through a lengthy reorganization meeting of the Ramsey governing
body, much of which, I'm afraid, was rather routine business.
As a Navy pilot many years ago, I flew patrol planes, usually on
missions lasting 10-12 hours. I once described that work as hours
of boredom interspersed with moments of terror. I hope your hour
or two of boredom today were interspersed with a few moments of
interest.

I will try to be brief. First, let me thank everyone who helped
make this meeting a success. I look forward to working for the next
four years with our borough administrator and borough clerk—two
of the many dedicated employees of Ramsey.

I am grateful to the elected officials who took time from their
busy schedules to be here today. Their presence is a promise, I
think, that Ramsey will have a voice in seats of government beyond
our borders.

My thanks, also, to the V.F.W. for leading us in paying our
respect to the flag of our nation. Active duty military personnel
and veterans of our armed forces often do not receive the respect
and honor they deserve. In times of crisis and war, we look to them
as our saviors, but in times of peace we, as a society, too often
forget the debt we owe our men and women in uniform. Military
service is no longer fashionable for the middle and upper classes
in our country. Of the 435 members of the United States Congress,
fewer than five have sons or daughters serving in the military.
Harvard University won't allow R.O.T.C. on its campus, yet it
receives federal research grants and support. Many other colleges
and universities ban military recruiters from their campuses.

That attitude is a failing of our society that I hope will one day be corrected.

My thanks, also, to Peter Del Vecchio, Conductor, and the Ramapo Wind Symphony for the musical selections today. Peter has also consented to help resurrect the Ramsey Fine Arts Council and serve as chairman of that newly constituted body. A community is more than just a means to fulfill basic governmental services, like police and fire protection, road repair and garbage collection. It is more than zoning ordinances, rules and regulations. A community must also have a soul, a spirit which gives voice to everything that is creative, inspirational and divine in the human condition. My administration will support the arts with commitment, expertise and money. We will look to you to support the arts with your enthusiasm, attendance at performances . . . and money.

I also wish to thank the Rev. Dr. Carol L. Brighton for delivering the Invocation. I am an ardent proponent of the separation of church and state, but I am also very much in agreement with the Founding Fathers of this nation, who recognized the importance of religion in our society. I look forward to working with the Rev. Dr. Brighton and other Ramsey clergy to enhance their participation in community affairs.

The election campaign is behind us, and now we turn our attention to governing. I promised to make Ramsey government more accessible and more responsive to residents. This meeting is being carried live on Cablevision, Channel 72. I will consult with my colleagues on the governing body to see if we can arrange a permanent plan of televising all future meetings of the governing body.

To my colleagues on the Ramsey governing body, I say thank you for making this meeting an expression of what government can be. Our borough form of government is a sharing of power between the mayor and the council. I embrace that concept. The election results have given me a mandate to put certain changes into place. But those changes must be made in consultation with the council. I plan to make haste slowly. To adopt a policy of gradualism, so that changes are well conceived, well understood, and well founded. I accept my responsibility as chief executive of this community to lead by example, to effect change by persuasion and reason, not by fiat, and to be responsive to the entire community, not just those who voted for me and my ideas.

In closing, let me leave you with words Miss Preische might have approved of. Miss Preische was my Latin teacher for three years here at Ramsey High School, about half a century ago. She was a wonderful teacher, as were just about every one of those men and women who helped form me into the person I am. She taught me a Latin phrase, which I remember to this day and which I will make the benchmark of my four years as mayor of Ramsey. *Acta, non verba.* Actions, not words. From this moment forward, measure me by my actions and the actions of my administration, not by my words.

Thank you, and good day.

Chapter 4

In My Father's Footsteps

A letter-to-the-editor, January 8, 2003

At 12:01 a.m. on January 1, 2003, I was sworn in as mayor of Ramsey, my hometown. It was one of the proudest moments in my life. Although a ceremonial swearing in would follow at the governing body's reorganization meeting on January 5th in the high school auditorium, I was particularly pleased that the "official" swearing in took place in the Ramsey Borough Hall.

What a wonderful old structure the Borough Hall is. Refurbished a few years back, it is almost youthful looking. Ascending the wide staircase in a 180-degree turn and entering the meeting room of the mayor and council, one is immediately taken by the Spartan utility of the room. A dais on the right stretches the length of the room and faces a phalanx of straight-back chairs. The walls are bare, but tastefully decorated in the neutral, unoffending beige of our times. The only thing missing is our heritage.

When I was growing up in Ramsey, I visited the Borough Hall often. For one thing, it housed the Ramsey Free Public Library, and I liked to read. By the time I reached sixth grade, I had read my way through the one-room library in the Ramsey Elementary School. And so I had graduated to the public library in the Borough Hall.

Although my choice of books was diverse—on any given day, I might have been seen leaving with a book on insects, another on Roman history, and a baseball novel for good measure—history was the subject matter I loved best.

The Borough Hall represented history to me. The building had been the elementary school for my father and all but one of his eight siblings. It was hard for me to disregard my father's elementary education experience, since my first, third, and fifth grade teachers had been his first, third, and fifth grade teachers. (Miss Hubbard, Miss Curnock, and Miss Petersen, respectively.) Years later, when my father was serving as Ramsey's Tax Assessor in the Borough Hall, he loved to relate to people how he had not progressed much in life—his office as Tax Assessor was formerly part of his third grade classroom.

The mayor and council meeting room in those days was a more somber chamber, but I didn't often venture into those upper reaches of the Borough Hall. I visited it once or twice when my father was sworn in as a councilman and, later, as council president. I don't remember much about those meetings, except that they were boring and too long. I do remember one striking feature of the room, though. Pictures of every Ramsey mayor were hung about the room, with little engraved plates giving their names and years of service. I think they were placed in order, ranging from John Finch, the first mayor after our incorporation as a borough in 1908, to Chester Smeltzer, who had risen to become a Bergen County Freeholder in the 1950's.

They all looked old to me then. Several had their hair parted down the middle, including Mayor "Buzz" Haring, who owned a butcher shop on Main Street. He took me bass fishing a few times, but the only thing I remember about that is getting up at the ungodly hour of 4:00 a.m. for the drive to the lake.

The portraits of Mayors Finch, Haring, Smeltzer and the others are now collecting dust in a basement storage room in the Borough Hall. For some reason, their presence was deemed inappropriate, not in keeping with the décor of the new council chambers. Too old-fashioned, I guess.

At one of our first meetings this year, I'm going to ask the council to reconsider their decision to consign my old friends to obscurity in the basement of the Borough Hall. Yes, maybe those portraits are a bit old-fashioned. But they are our heritage, and I, for one, would like to see them displayed again. Who knows—they may even inspire us to govern more effectively.

Chapter 5

This was the first of 54 "In the Arena" columns I wrote for the weekly Ramsey Suburban News. It appeared on February 19, 2003. The column provided a regular forum for my views on a range of issues, including the municipal budget, the War in Iraq, state and county government dysfunction, the fine arts, and Ramsey's and my own heritage. Some residents didn't like my outspokenness, especially on issues they felt were none of my business, like the school budget, which, in New Jersey, is managed by an independent Board of Education. Anything affecting residents of my town was fair game for comment, I thought. The school budget represented two-thirds of the property tax bill residents had to pay, and, in my mind, that put school issues at the top of the list of items that demanded critical discussion, not automatic approval.

Bull in a China Shop

A friend, whose opinion I value, recently advised me to tone down my efforts to reform Ramsey government. "Go slow," he said, "nobody likes a bull in a china shop." I see his point.

My first seven weeks in office have been eventful, to say the least. There was the borough attorney matter, which worked out okay. We were able to install a new attorney and save Ramsey taxpayers over $100,000 in 2003 alone. We'll easily save half a million dollars over the next four years. The council voted with me on that issue unanimously, and I appreciate their support. It demonstrated that partisanship can be put aside for the good of the community. The new borough attorney, by the way, has been doing an outstanding job.

Then, a former councilman, within days of leaving office, tried to get the Board of Adjustment to hire him as its attorney. During his 12 years in office, this councilman voted to confirm all nine current members of that Board, several for multiple terms. To me, that was a conflict of interest. I proposed, and the council passed, a resolution to bar former members of the governing body from taking any paid position with the Borough of Ramsey for one year after leaving office. The Board did the right thing in rejecting the former councilman. It is important to maintain the public's confidence in their government. Appearances of impropriety must be avoided.

I promised to speak out on all issues affecting Ramsey residents, including the school budget. Even at the risk of being labeled anti-education, which I am not, I cannot keep silent about something that accounts for 65% of the property taxes we pay. At the January meeting of the Board of Education, I stated publicly that its negotiating committee for the new teacher contract should take a serious look at pay and benefits.

In these difficult economic times, government employees—yes, even teachers and school administrators—have to know we cannot support four-, five-, or six-percent pay increases when the cost of living has averaged well below three percent for at least the last five years. Property taxes cannot continue their upward spiral, especially when unemployment is at its highest level in years and so many people are hurting. With costs escalating 20% or more a year and no relief in sight, free health insurance benefits for government employees and their families become less justifiable. The private sector is being forced to economize by asking employees to contribute toward this benefit. Government and school systems need to do the same.

I don't suggest that I have all the answers. Indeed, I rely heavily on the good sense and experience of my colleagues on the council—colleagues from both parties—and on the many fine employees of the Borough. But my training as a prosecutor has taught me to ask pointed questions.

For example, I have questions about the Board of Education's new school facilities proposal and the $26 million price tag. In a letter to the Board, I've posed my questions and will keep an open mind until I receive and review the response.

I rely also on what Ramsey residents tell me. Local government is now more accessible to the people. I have open office hours. Already, dozens of citizens have stopped by to express their thoughts and concerns, or just to chat. I've also received over 500 e-mails, phone calls and letters, all of which I personally answered—usually within 24 hours of receipt. I've found I can get by on four or five hours of sleep a night, so my e-mail responses will often show a time sent of 1:00 or 2:00 or even 3:00 a.m. I promise not to return phone calls at that hour.

Go slow? It is not in my nature, I'm afraid. I regret that I must disappoint my friend, though I shall try to break as few plates as possible.

Teddy Roosevelt, one of my heroes, often referred to the presidency as a "bully pulpit." What he meant, of course, was that it gave him tremendous freedom to speak out on any issue of importance. He did not squander his opportunity, as I shall not squander mine as mayor.

The Ramsey *Suburban News* has offered me this weekly column, for which I am very appreciative. There are no restrictions on subject matter, and I intend to range freely. I will strive to make my columns both interesting to read and relevant to our experience as citizens of the Borough of Ramsey, the State of New Jersey, and the United States of America.

My column will be called "IN THE ARENA," which history buffs will recognize as a phrase borrowed from one of Teddy Roosevelt's most famous speeches. (That speech appears in its entirety on my web site, www.mayormuti.com.)

In choosing that name for my column, I suppose I am making a statement of sorts—namely, that I will say what I think, without regard to political consequences. Please respond with your candid reactions, in letters to the editor or directly to me. My web site has a feedback form for your comments on any issue, be it the subject of one of my columns or an unrelated matter. It also has information on how you can contact me. I'm in my office at the borough hall every day; please try me there first. Each comment will receive a personal response from me, so let's hear from you.

Whether you agree with my point of view or not, I don't think you'll find my columns dull. I hope to provoke thought and discourse, but expect that critics will knock me around a bit. That's okay. If Roosevelt's "man in the arena" could take it, so can I.

Chapter 6

The Rule of Law

As a former prosecutor, I respect the rule of law; it is one of the most sacred principles of our great nation. Honoring that principle in the abstract is one thing, but adhering to it when the cause is unpopular and the central figure in the controversy detestable—that's another story.

In 1963 Thomas Trantino and an accomplice murdered two Lodi, New Jersey, police officers in a most brutal and depraved manner. The accomplice was killed in a subsequent shoot-out, but Trantino was captured. In 1964, he was tried, convicted, and sentenced to death. When the U.S. Supreme Court declared the death penalty statutes of several states, and, by implication, all other states with similar laws, unconstitutional in 1972, Trantino's death sentence was automatically commuted to life in prison.

Under New Jersey law in those days, life in prison did not mean life in prison. Trantino became eligible for parole in 25 years. The state parole board turned him down year after year. Finally, through the efforts of Trantino's pro bono defense attorney, Roger Lowenstein—who, by the way, taught me criminal procedure at Rutgers Law School—the N.J. Supreme Court ordered Trantino's release on parole.

I wrote two articles on this subject. The first appeared as an Op-Ed in The Record on January 7, 2001, before the Supreme Court had decided the case. The second appeared as a feature article in New Jersey Lawyer on February 19, 2001, after the Supreme Court issued its ruling. Not surprisingly, I took a view contrary to the popular will, praising the lawyer and jurist who stood up for the rule of law and condemning the politicians who lacked the backbone to lead their constituents in the right direction, the direction of honorable respect for our institutions. You know by now that I tend to look to history for parallels to our present situations. No different here, where the whole episode called to mind a heroic figure of the past—Sir Thomas More.

Even the Most Loathsome Defendants Deserve Fair Treatment Under the Law

Every once in a while, I observe someone who epitomizes my ideal of the lawyer as hero. Not an Atticus Finch, or a product of Grisham's or Turow's creative talent, but a real-life lawyer, slugging it out for a principle, no matter how reprehensible the client or unpopular the cause.

Roger Lowenstein is such a person.

Lowenstein represents Thomas Trantino, whose sadistic murder of two Lodi, New Jersey, police officers in 1963 has justly earned him the undying enmity of the victims' families. Convicted and sentenced to death in 1964, Trantino, like hundreds of other convicted murderers across the nation, escaped that fate when, in 1972, the United States Supreme Court struck down the death penalty statute of Georgia. The Court ruled that the manner in which the death penalty was being enforced constituted cruel and unusual punishment in violation of the Eighth Amendment. In short order the death penalty statutes of some 30-odd states were invalidated. Most states, including New Jersey, later passed capital punishment laws modified to satisfy the constitutionality concerns of a majority of the Court, but those new death penalty sanctions could not be applied retroactively. Trantino could not be executed.

In my opinion, the death penalty was being arbitrarily applied and deserved to be struck down, until safeguards could be instituted. Given the recent experience in Illinois and Texas, as reported by the *Chicago Tribune*, and problems in other states, like the malfunction of Florida's electric chair during an execution, one has to wonder whether we've progressed much since 1972, some 600 executions later.

Trantino's death sentence was commuted to life, which meant that he became eligible for parole in 25 years, less commutation time and work credits. Although Trantino had murdered two people and could have theoretically received two consecutive life sentences, the Bergen County Prosecutor charged both murders in the same count of the indictment. By that stroke of fortune, Trantino was eligible for parole in 1979.

After a few early missteps Trantino, by all accounts, became a model prisoner. But being eligible for parole doesn't mean that a prisoner is automatically entitled to release. He or she must first convince the Parole Board that the likelihood of continued criminal conduct after release on parole is remote and the public would not be endangered. Ironically, Trantino did just that on his second try. In 1980 the Board ordered his release, but only after a court determined how much Trantino would have to pay the victims' families in restitution.

The court refused to set a restitution amount. By that time, public outrage had galvanized. The Parole Board caved in to political pressure and reversed its decision. Any hope Trantino had for an early release ended.

Since then, Trantino's case has bounced back and forth between Parole Board and courts. Politicians, quick to spot a no-lose issue, eagerly joined the fray. With media lights glaring and loudspeakers blaring, they stand shoulder-to-shoulder with uniformed officers on the courthouse steps whenever Trantino's parole comes up for consideration.

When plans were being formulated to prepare for Trantino's release, one New Jersey state senator pressured prison officials by threatening to hold hearings on the parole process. The Department of Corrections discontinued its initiative in Trantino's behalf, and the senator called off his hearings. On another occasion, the Department of Corrections issued an order to move Trantino to a half-way house, an initial step in the parole release process. Amid the ensuing public outcry, that order was also rescinded.

Under the Parole Act of 1979, which controls the decision in Trantino's case, an eligible inmate must be released unless "there is a substantial likelihood that the inmate will commit a crime" if he is released on parole. The burden is on the side opposing parole to make its case.

Psychologists have flip-flopped on the question of Trantino's present threat to the public if he is released. In 1997, Judge Sylvia Pressler, a highly respected jurist in New Jersey, said: "There is absolutely nothing I can find in any of the background material, including the professional evaluations through the years, reasonably supporting the conclusion that Trantino will commit another crime if he is released under appropriate monitoring conditions. Indeed, everything on the record is to the contrary."

On June 9, 2000, the Appellate Division of the Superior Court ordered Trantino's release on parole. A unanimous three-judge panel ruled that the Parole Board's most recent decision to refuse parole was "not supported by substantial credible evidence in the record." The State appealed that ruling, and the matter is now under consideration by the New Jersey Supreme Court, which heard oral argument several months ago, but has not yet issued its decision.

True to form, State Senator Louis Kosco sponsored a state senate resolution urging the Supreme Court to overturn the lower court ruling, but his political maneuvering will not likely affect the high court's deliberations.

One hopes the New Jersey Supreme Court, which long enjoyed a nationwide reputation for integrity and jurisprudence under former Chief Justice Robert Wilentz, will be immune to the politics. Whatever the outcome, lawyers everywhere can feel proud about Roger Lowenstein's long, beautifully quixotic fight on behalf of a principle.

I am reminded of "A Man for All Seasons," the Oscar-winning film that starred Paul Scofield in the role of Thomas More. It portrayed More's struggle to keep himself and his family safe, in the face of King Henry VIII's wish to divorce Catherine of Aragon and marry Anne Boleyn. In Tudor England (and all of Christendom, for that matter) divorce was not permitted under law, even for kings. King Henry was adamant. He would have his woman, despite the law. He commanded Thomas More, his influential Chancellor, to publicly sanction the divorce and remarriage. In the film's most indelible scene, More's wife, daughter and son-in-law try to persuade him to accede to the King's demand. They plead with him to ignore the law just this once, for all their sakes.

More would not bend. The law is our refuge, he tells them. If we ignore first one law, then another for expediency, where do we go then for protection when the power of the State turns against us, "the laws all being flat."

No amount of political posturing, appeals to emotion or outright demagoguery should impede the rule of law. An appellate court has made a courageous decision to release Thomas Trantino, convicted double murderer, for the important reason that the law requires it. Thanks to the heroic efforts of one lawyer, we may once again see the triumph of this enduring principle of American jurisprudence.

Politicians and Trantino:
Searching for One Profile in Courage

The New Jersey Supreme Court's decision to grant convicted cop-killer Thomas Trantino parole, after he spends 12 months in a halfway house, had Bergen County politicians clambering all over themselves to duly register their opposition.

County Executive William "Pat" Schuber phoned in his outrage from Washington, D.C., where he was attending inaugural festivities. He called on then Governor Christie Whitman and her successor Donald DiFrancesco to pursue further appeals, but the U.S. Supreme Court, despite its recent toe-dipping in Florida electoral waters, is not likely to get involved in a purely intra-state controversy. Does Mr. Schuber know of a state tribunal higher than the New Jersey Supreme Court—a star chamber, perhaps, in which poll-takers render decisions unencumbered by legal technicalities like the U.S. Constitution and the rule of law?

State Senator Louis Kosco, who has made a career of Trantino-bashing, called the Court's decision "our worst nightmare." State Assemblyman Guy Talarico wondered aloud, "what's in the heads of these judges?" as he lamented their tendency to let justice cloud their thinking. State Assemblywoman Rose Heck dredged up Trantino's drug problem from the 1960's, ignoring the fact that the man has committed no infractions in more than 30 years.

Other state legislators, according to newspaper accounts, offered the almost prayerful suggestion that Trantino would screw up while in the halfway house and be returned to prison. Is this a portent of Trantino litigation to come? It is not a stretch to contemplate charges of parole violations, countercharges of planted drugs or similar misconduct, demands for new psychological evaluations, and other attempts to circumvent the Court's determination that political pandering in the matter of Thomas Trantino must cease.

Associate Justice Gary Stein wrote the 4-1 majority opinion of the Court. In language reminiscent of judicial giants long gone, Justice Stein said, "Carved into the stone of the facade of the United States Supreme Court building are these words: 'Equal Justice Under Law.' If courts ever permit agencies of government to create exceptions to the rule of law, applying it for the many but excepting the disfavored, we will have irreparably damaged the foundation of our democracy."

Magnificent and stirring words, indeed. Unfortunately, they fall on the deaf ears of today's politicians.

When was the last time we saw a politician take an unpopular stand simply because it was the right thing to do? Was it Daniel Patrick Moynihan, who thirty years ago decried the welfare cycle that kept inner-city blacks in abject poverty, only to be praised today for his foresight? Was it Harry Truman, who fifty years ago ended segregation in the military services by executive order despite the protestations of generals and admirals? Examples of such leadership are too few and too far between.

Today, we are awash in politicians too craven to stand up for a principle as sacred as the rule of law. Instead of taking us beyond emotionalism, they denounce the very institutions that form the bedrock of our government, simply to win votes. No less a hero than U.S. Senator John McCain has admitted to compromising his principles for the sake of political expediency. In the South Carolina Republican primary, McCain and every other major candidate supported that state's practice of flying the Confederate flag over its state house, notwithstanding the affront it presented to people of color. Only after the election did Mr. McCain acknowledge the wrongness of that practice and express his remorse for not having had the political backbone to denounce it when it mattered.

Maybe it is not the politicians who are at fault. Until we hold public officials accountable for their cowardly and shameless appeals to our baser instincts, until we acquire the purpose not only to admire political courage and integrity, but also to raise up those who display such qualities, we will get the kind of government we deserve.

Chapter 7

This second "In the Arena" column appeared on February 26, 2003.

Call Me a Tree Hugger

I love trees.

When my wife Lorraine and I first inspected the site of our present home in Ramsey, I was immediately taken by the beauty of the property. A half dozen Norwegian spruces towered above the Victorian house and its "lemonade" porch. One or two of them would be prime candidates for Rockefeller Center, if ever I would consent to cutting them down. Japanese maples, their forms as delicate as haiku, were scattered about. A large mulberry tree in the front yard brought back memories of the mulberry behind Micek's Bakery (now Allstate Insurance) I used to climb as a kid. But one tree in particular, a specimen white oak, closed the sale. It stands just over the property line—on my side, I'm glad to say.

I read about a way to estimate a tree's age by measuring its circumference four feet above ground level and multiplying the result by a factor based on tree species. I soon enlisted Lorraine in the Tree Huggers Brigade, and together we measured our prize. We discovered that our white oak is about 180 years old. It was a sapling when Thomas Jefferson and John Adams were writing letters to each other, reminiscing about the founding of our nation. Just the thought of that makes me happy.

My spirit is uplifted when I see a particularly beautiful treescape. I can't explain why. Perhaps it is some primordial instinct, a vestige of caveman ancestors taking sanctuary in a leafy glade. Joyce Kilmer would have found a kindred spirit in me as he walked along the Erie Lackawanna tracks in the days before the First World War. Though, I must admit, I *have* seen poems "as lovely as a tree."

I love all kinds of trees. The demise of the American elm was a tragedy of epic proportions, in my mind. We lost most of our elms in the Dutch elm disease epidemic of the 1960's and 1970's. A parasitic fungus gained a foothold in Ohio in 1930 and spread across the eastern United States, where the American elm was the most popular shade tree lining the Main Streets of countless small towns. The imported fungus blocked circulation in the defenseless elms, as effectively as super-sized Big Macs and fries clog our arteries. But unlike the human malady, the elm disease was contagious, carried from tree to tree by boring beetles and interlacing root systems.

Here and there, a few magnificent examples of *Ulmus americana* survive. People across the country, fellow tree huggers, are working to bring this tree species back from the brink of extinction. (Go to www.mayormuti.com for a link to Bruce Carley's wonderful web site, "Saving the American Elm." That site has numerous links to other sites on the same subject, along with photos of the American elm that will take your breath away.)

Sometimes we lose trees for less understandable reasons. Like a developer clear-cutting to facilitate construction, when a little extra care would have preserved much of the tree cover. I've even heard of homeowners wanting to take down trees because they were tired of raking leaves.

Some would say, "So what. It's a free country, isn't it? People should be able to do whatever they want with their own property."

That argument has a certain amount of appeal. Government too often intrudes into areas it should keep its nose out of. But there are instances when we welcome government rule-making and intervention—to quell disputes between neighbors, for example. Zoning laws keep one property owner from infringing on the rights of another.

We require structures like garages, decks and such to be "set back" from adjacent properties, so a neighbor doesn't feel crowded. We establish minimum lot sizes and maximum densities to preserve open space on commercial and residential properties and to promote good drainage. If a neighbor were to blacktop his entire lot, rainwater might run off into your basement. Ordinances requiring preservation of "green space" and controlling soil movement are designed to forestall such occurrences.

So you see, we willingly give up rights over our domain for good reason. Why not an ordinance to protect trees?

We already have one of sorts, but it may need strengthening. Our present ordinance in Ramsey requires property owners to obtain permission from the shade tree commission before cutting down more than six trees having a four-inch or greater diameter in any 12-month period. No permission is needed to remove trees less than four inches in diameter in any quantity; similarly, a property owner can remove six trees of any size every 12 months without permission. Under our present tree ordinance, someone buying my home on Church Street could take down the Jefferson/ Adams oak for firewood or some equally paltry reason. Or, for no reason.

I began to think about this issue thanks to a resident calling me to suggest controls over indiscriminate cutting of mature trees. Then, I read a newspaper story about the Wyckoff governing body taking up an ordinance with a similar purpose. It sounded like a good idea, so I asked the chairman of our shade tree commission to consider the issue and make recommendations to the planning board and borough council.

The commission will study the advisability of placing controls over tree cutting, but with reasonable limitations. For example, it may recommend that trees of a certain size or age be protected, or that buffer zones be established by regulating trees near property lines. Any proposed ordinance must have flexibility to allow the zoning board of adjustment or planning board to make exceptions when need for a variance is established by a property owner. In any event, the Ramsey governing body will await the findings of our shade tree commission and planning board. If an ordinance is proposed, residents will be given ample notice and opportunity to comment before its adoption.

The mayor and council have a duty to enact laws that promote the public health, safety, and welfare. In grade school, we all learned about the importance of trees. How they prevent soil erosion, provide shade, and sustain life by transforming carbon dioxide into the very oxygen we breathe. Trees are a community resource and treasure; we should do a better job of protecting them. Jefferson would have called that a self-evident truth.

Chapter 8

Early in 2003, I supported President Bush in his call for war against Iraq. The president had made his case, I thought, that our national security interests were threatened. Then, we learned more about the Bush administration's efforts to mislead the public and manufacture a causus belli, and I took a different view, speaking out against the war. But this article, published on March 5, 2003, just before the war was launched, urged my constituents to get behind our Commander-in-Chief.

"Dulce et Decorum Est"

The day after President Bush's State of the Union address, a woman called me at Borough Hall, where I work as Ramsey's first Democratic mayor in 16 years. A supporter of mine, she wanted to know if I was going to provide a bus for anti-war demonstrators to travel to Washington, D.C., to join a protest march. Geopolitics, it seems, has gone local.

I told her busing to a political rally was not a proper use of taxpayers' money. I also said I agreed with the president's assessment of the danger Iraq posed. She was irate.

"You call yourself a Democrat?" she said. "How can you condone the killing of innocent women and children?"

Civilians die in war, and U.S. forces have killed their share. Most were unavoidable, but we have had our ignoble moments. *My Lai* in Viet Nam and *No Gun Ri* in Korea come to mind. Those were aberrations, I truly believe. No other nation in history has been more careful to avoid civilian casualties than we have been. But they have happened before and will happen again in Iraq. When war comes, we will see daily CNN reports of tragic mistakes that test our resolve. But we cannot allow civilian casualties to detract from this noble purpose. We must protect our national interests.

I support President Bush's handling of the Iraq crisis, although I would have preferred less saber-rattling and fewer avowals of "time is running out." We've drawn so many lines in the sand that our words are becoming meaningless. Secretary of State Colin Powell's diplomatic initiatives were undermined by more hawkish elements in the Bush administration. It now appears that war is all but inevitable.

I first came across Wilfred Owen's grim and haunting poem in high school and have re-read it many times since. The full Latin phrase, from which the poem's title is taken, is *Dulce et Decorum Est Pro Patria Mori*. Roughly translated, it means, "It is fitting and proper to die for one's country."

Owen captured the stark reality of death by gas attack in World War I. Here is an excerpt.

Dim through the misty panes and thick green light,
As under a green sea, I saw him drowning.
In all my dreams before my helpless sight
He plunges at me, guttering, choking, drowning.

Through the convulsions of a dying soldier, the poet asks whether it can ever be "fitting and proper" to sacrifice life for a national purpose. Today, as we face a potential foe likely to use chemical and biological weapons, Owen's question is especially relevant.

My answer is yes—sometimes it *is* necessary to spend lives in a noble cause. And sometimes it is a tragic waste.

It was a waste when President Clinton sent an inadequate force to Somalia and allowed an American boy to be dragged through Mogadishu by cheering hoodlums and did nothing about it. It was a waste when Bush the Elder left Saddam Hussein in power, free to annihilate Kurds and Shiites who had risen up in response to our empty promise of support. It was a waste when four presidents—Eisenhower, Kennedy, Johnson and Nixon—failed to recognize the lessons of history and undertook to intervene in a civil war in Viet Nam whose outcome posed no threat to our national security.

The situation in Iraq is more complicated than earlier military actions. Anyone who denies the existence of this real threat to our national security is following the "ostrich" method of foreign policy. Hussein has guided missile capabilities and has used chemical weapons before. He has attempted to build nuclear weapons using French technology, a process that was cut short by a preemptive Israeli air strike. Given the chance, he will certainly try again. Indeed, if reports of undetected tunnels beneath Baghdad are true, he may already have nukes. I shudder to think how many Soviet nuclear weapons are missing and how many of their nuclear physicists are now at work in rogue countries like Iraq.

President Bush is a likeable man, but I find his performance in office spotty. He displayed leadership after 9-11 in the war against terrorism, a war that seems to be taking a backseat now. In certain areas, though, he has not distinguished himself. North Korea, for one. President Clinton had opened a dialog with the North Koreans, who were anxious to continue the new relationship with Bush. Mr. Bush rejected any overtures to the Communist state, labeling it one of the "axis of evil" countries. That was a mistake, we are now learning. The North Koreans have reactivated a nuclear reactor, may already have several nuclear weapons, and are testing missiles. We are now trying to buy off the North Koreans with promises of financial aid.

I hope President Bush sees us through this crisis with wisdom and courage. The brave young people we are about to send in harm's way must have a united home front. Let's get behind them and our president. I respect every American's right of free speech and assembly, but there comes a time to stand with our leaders against the enemy. That time is now.

Chapter 9

This piece appeared as the featured article in The Record's Opinion section on Sunday, April 14, 2002. The Record, home-based in Bergen County, has the second largest circulation in New Jersey. It has been a favorite outlet for my writings on a wide range of subjects.

I'd taught a death penalty course at Fairleigh Dickinson University in Teaneck. That, along with my experience as a prosecutor, got me this particular assignment.

This article received a lot of attention. Many readers assumed I was an opponent of capital punishment, but, in fact, my views on the subject are not that simple. I favor a limited-scope death penalty, with strict safeguards in its application and finality in the appeals process—but that's an article for another day.

More than five years later, the subject is still one of controversy in New Jersey. As of this writing, a bill to abolish the death penalty, which the governor has promised to sign, awaits legislative action.

Rethinking Capital Punishment

On Monday Ray Krone stepped into the Arizona sunshine a free man, after twice being convicted of murder and spending the last ten years in prison. Krone was sentenced to death in 1992 for murdering and sexually assaulting Kim Ancona, a Phoenix cocktail waitress. When that conviction was overturned on a technicality, Krone was retried before a second jury and again convicted, but this time his lawyers were successful in avoiding the death penalty for their client. Krone, who had spent three years on death row, was sentenced to life in prison.

The only significant evidence against Krone in both trials, according to defense attorney Christopher Plourd, was bite marks on the victim's left breast. Prosecutors at both trials presented the same forensic expert, who testified that the marks were consistent with Krone's crooked tooth structure. In other words, the expert said Krone made the bite marks.

"We presented three defense experts who testified that Ray's teeth didn't make those bite marks," Plourd said, "but the jury chose to believe the state's expert."

The jury was wrong both times. DNA evidence conclusively proved that another man, Kenneth Phillips, committed the crime. Phillips lived a short distance from the bar where Kim Ancona worked, but was not even considered a suspect at the time. He later was imprisoned for assaulting a minor and, under Arizona law, his DNA profile was added to a state data base. Krone's attorneys obtained a court order to search that data base using procedures not available in 1992, and Phillips' DNA proved to match the DNA left at the murder scene.

Prosecutors were so convinced of Phillips' guilt and Krone's innocence that they immediately went before a Maricopa County Superior Court judge to ask for Krone's release. A hearing is scheduled later this month to officially dismiss the charges, but it is a mere formality.

Ray Krone became the 100th former death row inmate to be released since 1973, according to the Death Penalty Information Center, a Washington, D.C., group that gets most of its funding from the J. Roderick MacArthur Foundation of Niles, Illinois. That same foundation also funds The MacArthur Justice Center, a non-profit public interest law firm affiliated with the University of Chicago Law School, and the American Civil Liberties Union—both fervent death penalty foes.

Richard C. Dieter, executive director of the Death Penalty Information Center, concedes that his group has been "mostly critical" of the death penalty as it is currently administered in the United States, but contends that DPIC's function is research, analysis and education. "We have not taken a position on the death penalty per se," he said in a recent interview. Yet, Dieter is quick to point out that problems with the death penalty over the last 25 years have not been fixed. "Arbitrariness and racial bias are difficult to root out," he said.

The 25- to 30-year time frame, roughly speaking, is generally accepted as the "modern era" in capital punishment jurisprudence. It stems from the U.S. Supreme Court's decision in Furman v. Georgia, a 1972 case that declared the Georgia and Texas death penalty statutes unconstitutional and, by extension, outlawed capital punishment throughout the United States. Georgia redrafted its death penalty law to address the Court's concerns, and that new statute, which passed Constitutional muster in 1976, became the model for 37 other states. But it could not be applied retroactively.

As a result of Furman, 613 death row inmates in 30 states had their death sentences commuted to life imprisonment by the stroke of a pen. Among them was Thomas Trantino, whose recent release on parole ended a decades-long fight by Bergen County law enforcement, politicians and residents to keep the convicted cop-killer behind bars.

Three of the Furman prisoners were later found to be not guilty of the crimes for which they were condemned to death. In other words, had the Supreme Court not acted, three innocent men would have been executed.

[In New Jersey, news of the exoneration of the 100th wrongly convicted death-row inmate touched off a Trenton protest last week, with foes of capital punishment calling on state legislators to pass a bill that would stay executions until a study could be conducted on the death penalty's effectiveness. The bill is currently sitting in committee.]

The prospect of a mistaken execution did not always alarm society's civil libertarians. John Stuart Mill, steadfast defender of 19th century British liberalism, argued in Parliament against a proposed measure abolishing the death penalty. Mill considered execution to be the more humane punishment, rather than a life sentence in prisons of the day. "[T]he short pang of a rapid death," he said, was less severe than confinement "in a living tomb." As for the occasional mistaken execution, Mill found the risk acceptable. "The man would have died at any rate," Mill said, "not so very much later on average . . . and with a considerably greater amount of bodily suffering."

Today, the execution of an innocent person is everyone's worst nightmare—pro-death penalty and anti-death penalty factions, alike. That may be the reason, perhaps, why Death Penalty Information Center's so-called "innocence list"—the running tally, now totaling 100, of inmates released from death row in the modern era—has attracted the attention of the media and public, not to mention the wrath of death penalty advocates.

"It's nothing more than a bogus public relations ploy," said Dudley Sharp, resource director of Justice For All, a staunch pro-death penalty group operating out of Houston, Texas. Harris County, Texas, along with its political subdivision, Houston, are considered by many to be the death penalty capital of the United States. Its prosecutors have the distinction of consigning more convicted murderers to death row than any other county in the nation.

The Harris County D. A.'s office recently concluded one of the more notorious death penalty trials in recent years. It involved Andrea Pia Yates, found guilty of murder in the drowning her five children. Mothers who kill their own children rarely face the death penalty. Susan Smith in South Carolina was another exception. Yates, with a documented history of mental illness, had pleaded insanity, but D.A. Chuck Rosenthal—elected, as all district attorneys in Texas are—said that "citizens of Harris County ought to be able to consider the full range of punishments in this case, including the death penalty." The jury that convicted Yates decided on a life sentence rather than the death penalty.

Some have speculated that D.A. Rosenthal's severe treatment of Andrea Yates, a middle class white, was designed to counterbalance the number of poor black defendants who are exposed to the death penalty in his county each year.

Justice For All's Dudley Sharp is the author of numerous pro-death penalty monographs, in which he attempts to debunk hot-button anti-death penalty issues like racial bias and mental retardation. One of Sharp's favorite targets is DPIC's innocence list. Sharp makes the point that most of the so-called "innocent" death row inmates on DPIC's list were released on a legal technicality, not because they were proven to be innocent. "This debate," Sharp says, referring to the dreaded prospect of a mistaken execution, "is not about legal innocence; it is and always has been about factual innocence, meaning, 'I didn't do it.'"

DPIC's list of 100 inmates released from death row is vastly inflated with "legally" innocent defendants, according to Sharp—defendants who may very well be guilty, but who got off because of a legal loophole. Nevertheless, Sharp allows that perhaps 30 factually innocent people may have been sentenced to death since 1973. If one considers that approximately 7,000 convicted murderers have received the death penalty in that time frame, 30 mistaken verdicts, or 0.4% of the total, is "an acceptable margin of error," Sharp said. Moreover, not one of these so-called innocents has been executed, a fact which Sharp offers as proof that the system works.

Richard Dieter concedes that "there hasn't yet been definitive proof of an innocent person being executed." But the DPIC executive director suggests that states have no incentive to open their evidence files regarding executed murderers. Many states, including New Jersey, require that evidence from homicide cases be retained indefinitely. It would be possible, theoretically, to gather DNA from a 30-year old murder case and prove conclusively whether an executed defendant actually committed the crime.

There's no percentage in states cooperating with an effort that may lead to their being publicly embarrassed, according to Dieter. Indeed, there is movement afoot in some states to outlaw inquiries into old murder cases with no living defendant.

Dieter downplays Sharp's distinction between factually innocent and legally innocent people on DPIC's list. "We don't just add a case because a defense attorney thinks his or her client didn't do the crime," Dieter said in a recent interview. He went on to describe the criteria his organization uses before a case is added to the innocence list.

A defendant whose conviction is overturned by a judge must be further exonerated in one of three ways: he must be acquitted at a new trial, or the prosecutor must drop the charges against him, or a governor must grant an absolute pardon. All 100 former death row inmates on the innocence list have been exonerated in one of those three ways, according to Dieter.

But Sharp doesn't buy it. "For death penalty opponents," he

says, "the innocence issue has become but another distortion-based campaign."

Coincidentally, there is another list of 100 released defendants that has also received great public attention recently. Even Dudley Sharp seems to treat it with respect. The Innocence Project, a Cardozo Law School operation cofounded in 1992 by attorney and DNA expert Barry Scheck, has been instrumental in overturning convictions and setting free 100 wrongfully convicted men, accused primarily of sex crimes. This feat has been accomplished solely through the use of DNA evidence, which Scheck champions as highly reliable.

The relevance of Scheck's and co-founder Peter Neufeld's work to the death penalty issue is this. The 100 men freed by scientifically precise DNA evidence had been convicted by other evidence previously thought to be reliable. Evidence like eye-witness testimony, hair and fiber comparison tests, and even confessions by the exonerated defendants, themselves. In other words, 100 juries listened to victims identify their assailants, scientific experts render opinions, and police officers testify that defendants had confessed to them, then unanimously decided on the guilt of those 100 men beyond a reasonable doubt. And they were wrong 100 times.

Even fingerprint evidence, a previously sacrosanct law enforcement tool, has had its reliability questioned recently. U.S. District Court Judge Louis H. Pollak said prosecution experts could not testify that fingerprints found at a crime scene "matched" those of a defendant. In a ruling that could have had far reaching effects on the way criminal investigations and prosecutions are conducted, the judge ruled there was no scientific basis for experts to reach so definitive a conclusion as an exact "match." Asked by prosecutors to reconsider his decision, Judge Pollak reversed himself two months later. "I just changed my mind," he said.

DNA technology "points out flaws in the system," said Steven Hawkins, executive director of the National Coalition to Abolish the Death Penalty. Among the flaws Hawkins cites are "mistaken eyewitness identifications, unreliable jailhouse snitches, prosecutorial misconduct and exculpatory evidence that may come to light years after the crime."

Hawkins makes no claim of impartiality in the death penalty

debate. His organization, founded with the support of the American Civil Liberties Union in 1976 when the Supreme Court reinstated the death penalty, has five thousand members and a thousand national, state and local affiliates. NCADP's one and only purpose, according to Hawkins, is abolishment of the death penalty.

Hawkins was asked whether the system was fixable. "That's the big question," he replied, pointing to no less an authority than former Supreme Court Justice Harry Blackmun, one of four justices in the minority when Furman v. Georgia was decided in 1972. That is, he voted to uphold the death penalty.

But in 1994, Justice Blackmun had a change of heart. In a capital case dissent, Blackmun wrote, "From this day forward, I shall no longer tinker with the machinery of death. Rather than continue to coddle the Court's delusion that the desired level of fairness has been achieved . . . , I feel morally and intellectually obligated simply to concede that the death penalty experiment has failed."

Justice Lewis Powell Jr., who voted with Blackmun to uphold the death penalty on numerous occasions, also expressed regret in 1994 over those votes. Powell told his biographer, "I would [now] vote the other way in any capital case."

Both Powell and Blackmun are long gone from the court, of course. But there may be further evidence of weakening support for capital punishment on the nation's highest court. In a July 2001 speech to an organization of women lawyers in Minnesota, Justice Sandra Day O'Connor, by her past decisions a firm supporter of the death penalty's constitutionality, said, "If statistics are any indication, the system may very well be allowing some innocent defendants to be executed."

Justice O'Connor was surely mindful of the situation in Illinois. In January 2000 Republican Governor George Ryan, a conservative death penalty supporter, declared a moratorium on executions in that state. Ryan's action came on the heels of hard-hitting investigative reporting by Chicago Tribune reporters Ken Armstrong and Steve Mills.

They examined all 285 death penalty cases in Illinois since capital punishment was restored in 1977. During that time period, Illinois had exonerated and released 13 men from death row, one more than it had executed. In a five-part series published in late 1999, Armstrong and Mills found "a system so plagued by unprofessionalism, imprecision and bias that they have rendered the state's ultimate form of punishment its least credible."

The reporters, who reviewed trial and appellate transcripts and interviewed witnesses, defendants and attorneys, learned that 33 defendants sentenced to die had been represented by lawyers subsequently disbarred or suspended from practice. In 46 cases, prosecutors had relied on evidence from jailhouse snitches, typically the most untrustworthy of witnesses. In 35 cases, a black defendant was sentenced to die by an all white jury, a result that could only have been achieved by prosecutors carefully skirting rules established by the Supreme Court to prevent such occurrences.

Indeed, ten percent of all Illinois death penalty convictions had been overturned by appellate courts because of some form of prosecutorial overreaching—not the most ringing endorsement of a profession whose highest ethical obligation in every jurisdiction of this country is not just to convict, but to see justice done.

Yet, in spite of much recent coverage of death penalty errors, the public continues to support capital punishment by a significant margin. In response to a May 2001 Gallup poll question, "Do you favor the death penalty for those convicted of murder," 65% of respondents answered, "Yes." A post-September 11, 2001, poll saw that support rise to 68%, a relatively small increase considering the devastating loss of innocent life on that date.

Diann Rust-Tierney, director of ACLU's Capital Punishment Project, suggests that "the public supports the death penalty in theory, but the more the public understands how it operates in practice, the more that support erodes." Indeed, when life without parole is offered as an alternative to the death penalty, public support drops below 50%.

Ms. Rust-Tierney is right in one other regard. The death penalty is imposed in roughly 10% of cases in which the defendant has been declared eligible for capital punishment. In other words, when holding the life of a fellow human being in their hands—someone whom they have just convicted of a brutal, egregious murder—juries can agree unanimously to impose a death sentence in just one out of every ten cases.

Justice Thurgood Marshall put the matter more bluntly in his concurring opinion in the Furman case. The public supports the death penalty, he said, because it is ignorant of the facts. If the public only knew, he argued, that the death penalty does not deter better than long terms of imprisonment, that its implementation is inhumane and that it is administered unfairly, "the great mass of citizens . . . would conclude that the death penalty is immoral and therefore unconstitutional."

Justice Marshall's prediction has, so far, not been realized. Neither have Justice Blackmun's or Justice Powell's personal reversals on the death penalty turned the tide of public support. States continue to tinker with the death penalty in an honest effort to make it fairer.

Even Texas, the undisputed leader in executions since 1976, passed laws last spring, after former Governor George W. Bush's departure for Washington, to improve legal representation of indigent defendants and to mandate DNA testing in capital cases. The legislature passed another bill to block the execution of mentally retarded defendants, something 18 other death penalty states and the federal government now prohibit, but Governor Rick Perry vetoed that measure.

Recent efforts to improve death penalty laws, like those in Texas, are just "a drop in the bucket," says ACLU's Diann Rust-Tierney. "Why should we keep putting money into fixing the car when it's never going to run?" she asks.

Richard Dieter of the Death Penalty Information Center characterized this 100th exoneration involving Ray Krone as a "wake-up call," a warning that "states are taking unnecessary risks with innocent lives."

If recent statistics are any indication, the public appetite for the death penalty may, in fact, be subsiding. Justice Department statistics show a decline in executions two years running. After a modern era peak of 98 in 1999, executions dropped to 85 in 2000 and 66 in 2001. The number of death sentences being imposed by juries and judges, for that matter, is also declining significantly. Death sentences decreased for the third straight year in 2000, when just 214 death sentences were imposed, the fewest since 1982. The final tally for 2001 was not available as of this writing.

Eroding public trust in government and other once sacred

institutions—like science, for example—may be spreading to the courtrooms of America.

The reality of junk science being used to convict innocent defendants came crashing down on even the most tough-on-crime advocates recently when the Federal Bureau of Investigation discredited the work of an Oklahoma City police scientist. Joyce Gilchrist had analyzed evidence in approximately 3,000 Oklahoma criminal cases from 1980 to 1993. In those cases, Ms. Gilchrist testified for the prosecution regarding blood, hair and fiber comparisons, matched results to defendants, and helped the state obtain countless convictions. Last spring, the F.B.I. said her work, either in the lab or courtroom, proved to be false in five of eight cases investigated.

Oklahoma Governor Frank Keating, himself a former prosecutor, ordered an immediate review of every felony conviction in which Ms. Gilchrist had any involvement. That process continues even now. Eventually, through new trials in some cases, outright dismissals in others, things will get sorted out, but the cost to Oklahoma taxpayers will be in the millions.

Another group will bear the greater cost, however. Scientist Joyce Gilchrist's testimony was instrumental in the conviction of 23 Oklahoma defendants sentenced to die by lethal injection. For 11 of those men, the inquiry into Ms. Gilchrist's credibility comes too late.

Chapter 10

This article was published in The New York Times on Sunday, December 2, 2001. It relates to my experience of being fired as Deputy First Assistant Prosecutor in August 2000 and trying to regain my dignity and self-respect in the aftermath. Writing the piece and having it accepted for publication by a newspaper like the New York Times helped me to cope with this painful time in my life.

Left High-Minded and Dry

—Paying Dearly for Playing the Game of Life by the Rules—

I was fired from my job as chief administrator of a law enforcement agency two months after turning sixty—just 10 months shy of qualifying for health benefits during my retirement and two years shy of maximizing my pension.

My boss, a political appointee and head of the agency, wanted to spend $7 million of public funds to buy and renovate an office building. I had doubts about the need—we were having difficulty coming up with people and functions to fill the extra space. With the crime rate in a decade-long decline, we should have been finding ways to downsize, not expand. I tried to discuss these reservations, but my boss turned a deaf ear.

After a cursory review, the county governing body approved the project. I agonized, then was stricken with and succumbed to an attack of high-mindedness. I wrote county officials a letter explaining why the building wasn't justified and asking them to give it closer scrutiny. I got the ax that same day.

My wife took it hard. We'd just purchased another house, an old Victorian we fell in love with, and had not yet sold our existing home, so we were carrying two mortgages. "What are we going to do," she whispered, as I held her in my arms that first night. I told her not to worry, that I'd find a job quickly. But it was just whistling past the proverbial graveyard. The self-assurance I had always felt, the confidence that my abilities and work ethic would see me through, vanished that night.

I had always worked, ever since I was tall enough to operate the soda fountain in my father's small-town luncheonette. While in high school, I worked nights and weekends at the local Howard Johnson's. My Dad's early training made me a star in that 28-flavor world. In college, I waited tables and ushered at movies and football games. While in the service stationed ashore, I sold encyclopedias door-to-door during my off-duty hours, Navy pay being what it was in those days.

Putting together a resume at the computer the next day, I felt my confidence return with each bold entry. Anybody would be nuts, I thought, not to want the guy I was describing on the screen.

- 1964 Annapolis graduate, B.S. degree
- 1964-69 Navy pilot
- 1971 Harvard Business School graduate, M.B.A. degree
- 1980 Rutgers Law School graduate, J.D. degree

I had nineteen years as a lawyer, with over 500 trials and a win percentage in the high nineties, and fourteen years as a senior manager in business and government. I couldn't wait to get my resumes out. I'd need help, I thought, handling calls and sifting through job offers.

I was not disheartened by the lack of immediate response. But after enduring a silent phone for a few weeks, I decided to be sensible about applying for unemployment compensation. It wasn't something I wanted to do. I knew it was an entitlement, that I had been paying into the fund all my life without drawing out a dime. Nevertheless, as a child of the Forties and Fifties, I couldn't help feeling a welfare-like stigma.

I pored over want ads. Tuesdays were best for *The Wall Street*

Journal. Lots of executive positions suited to my education and experience. Sundays were best for *The New York Times, The Record and The Star-Ledger.* At first, I sent out cover letters and resumes in those fancy Priority Mail envelopes at $3.20 each, hoping recipients would give special attention to my mailings. The phone remained silent, however, and I soon switched to the 34-cent method of communication.

Polite rejection letters began to arrive, with soothing words about someone fitting needs more closely and promises to keep my resume "on file." Many didn't bother to respond. As more and more companies announced layoffs to cope with the worsening economy, I cringed at the new competition each cutback would represent. But I kept at it.

The Internet looked useful, so I registered at several Web sites. One, Monster.com, promised over 400,000 job openings. I put my resume on line, headed with attention-grabbing words to lure employers who troll the data base. I used "Senior Administrator with Harvard MBA and law degree" as my hook. So far, twenty potential employers have looked at it. No phone calls, though. I may have to re-bait my hook. In a dark humor moment, I thought of using the ubiquitous Depression-era supplication, "Will Work for Food."

Recently, a friend, upset over my predicament, lashed out at me for what he perceived to be a self-inflicted wound. "What were you thinking?" he said. "Did you think anybody gives a damn about wasting the public's money? Why didn't you just keep your mouth shut, let them do what they want to do, and retire in two years with your pension and benefits intact?"

I often ask myself those same questions. When I recall the lessons my parents taught me and the values instilled in me at Annapolis and in the service, I feel proud about my actions, despite the personal cost. But late at night, when sleep is difficult and I find myself thinking about the sadness in my wife's eyes and her unspoken reproach for having thrown away our financial security over a selfish need "to do my duty," I am not so sure.

I've cleaned out the deferred compensation account I started years ago for our retirement. That old Victorian my wife and I bought turned out to have an unexpected feature. There is a bottomless pit in the rear yard, and every week or so, I have to go back there and throw money into it. While my fortunes may have taken a turn for the worse, I have been able to bring happiness to others. George, my electrician, and Tony, my plumber, and Rich, my carpenter, and Artie, my roofer, all had a very good year.

Chapter 11

No subject disturbs New Jersey homeowners more than their property taxes—the highest in the nation. There are three components to property tax bills: the municipal budget, used to operate local government; the school budget; and the local share of the County budget. Of these, the local governing body directly controls only the municipal budget.

Early in my tenure as mayor, I wanted to make the public aware of the budget process and wrote about it extensively. These next two pieces appeared as separate "In the Arena" columns during the budget season in the spring of 2003.

The Facts of Life about Property Taxes—Part I

Immediately after this year's budget resolution is introduced, a flyer with highlights will be mailed to every resident. But as we all know, the devil is in the details. And details are what everyone will have access to. For the first time in Ramsey's history, our full budget (all 46 pages) will be posted on the borough web site. We will also have five copies on reserve at the Ramsey Free Public Library for those who are not online. Finally, take-home copies will be available at the Borough Clerk's office for the copying fee set by ordinance last year.

The borough council and I will do our utmost to keep the municipal portion of your tax bill in check. Besides finding less expensive ways to do things, we can manage for a while because our surplus has replenished itself, to about $5.8 million. But don't expect that to continue for long. I think we need to gradually reduce our surplus to the $2-3 million range, which will be an adequate reserve for contingencies. A surplus, after all, represents over collection of taxes—money we received from taxpayers ahead of time. Governments with too much money tend to be wasteful governments. When we need more money to operate, we should be required to ask you for it *when* we need it, and to justify to you *why* we need it. Within a year or two, though, municipal taxes will begin to creep upward, despite our best efforts to rein in costs and cut waste. It is just a fact of life—an unpleasant one, but a fact nonetheless.

You've heard often enough that Ramsey is almost totally developed. There are a few vacant tracts of land remaining, and I want to see how we can protect those parcels from over development. But the economic reality of our tax ratable base is abundantly clear. With limited new taxpayers coming into Ramsey in the future, those of us who are already here will have to bear the increased costs of government—municipal, county and schools.

I have a few ideas about reducing the cost of municipal government, to stave off the inevitable day when taxes must be increased. For example, we must take what will surely be an unpopular stand with our borough employees. We must learn how to say no to them, and it pains me greatly to have to do that. For the most part, they are wonderful, hardworking people, who have their own problems trying to raise families and make ends meet. But we can't keep agreeing to salary increases far in excess of annual cost of living adjustments, or to free medical insurance for the entire family.

The published COLA figure has averaged under 2% for the past five years. How then can we justify giving 4 or 5% salary increases to borough employees every year? Especially with unemployment rates at their highest level in years and with so many of our residents hurting. Every employee is entitled to earn a fair salary, and perhaps some adjustments are necessary to insure fairness and equity in our pay schedules. But beyond making those adjustments where indicated, we must strive to keep pay increases at or below 3%.

The cost of health insurance benefits for our full time employees will soar to $1.3 million in 2003, about a 20% increase over last year—the third such increase in as many years. We pay $14,000 per employee to cover health and dental insurance on the family plan. Ramsey police officers have a more expensive plan as their benefit. (Why, I don't know—but I'm working to change that.) The cost to provide free health and dental benefits is over $16,000 per police officer on the family plan. Single employee coverage is significantly less.

The corporate world and just about every other non-government employer are requiring employees to participate in the cost of health insurance. I get my health insurance through my wife's employer, for example; but she has to pay an extra $90 per week out of her paycheck to obtain coverage for me. It's still a bargain, but the point is that almost everyone else is bearing part of the burden. If I have my way, Ramsey employees will move closer to the real world when it comes to health insurance benefits. I am personally involved in negotiations with our five employee unions, and health insurance givebacks will be a requirement of any new labor contract. I will insist on it.

In January, I appeared before the Ramsey Board of Education and made my feelings known on health insurance and salary increases in their budget. The BOE is in the midst of negotiating a new labor contract with teachers, and I urge them to be firm in their approach to pay and benefits.

We may be able to afford the cost of health insurance this year, or next year. But what about five or ten years from now. If we continue down this path, we will be eaten alive by the cost of this benefit. I cannot and will not allow that to happen during my tenure as mayor of Ramsey, no matter what the political consequences.

Undoubtedly, I shall incur the wrath of teachers, police, and other government employees because of my stand on these issues, but I do not despair over the possibility of being a one-term mayor. Don't get me wrong—I love this job. But I won't get down from my bully pulpit to keep it.

The Facts of Life about Property Taxes—Part II

Municipal taxes will increase this year by a modest amount—2.7%. On a home assessed at $460,000, that translates to an annual increase of $50.60 for the municipal portion of your tax bill. Over the next three years, barring any unforeseen circumstances, we project an average annual increase in municipal taxes of about 3.25 %.

Some would say: "Why increase taxes at all? Times are tough." And they would probably receive a sympathetic response from most residents. While maintaining a flat tax rate will always be popular, it is not always the best policy—not when so many economic challenges face us. In 2000, 2001, and 2002, the municipal tax rate remained flat, but, of course, expenditures went up in each of those years, too. We paid for those increased expenditures with surplus. For example, in last year's budget, the prior administration used $4.43 million in surplus to balance the budget and maintain the same tax rate as the year before. That was the highest use of surplus in Ramsey's history. This year, we will use $2.45 million in surplus, almost two million less. Expenses must be covered some way, either with surplus or increased taxes.

Surplus represents money the borough collects from you in advance of needing it. Keeping some surplus in these uncertain times is prudent policy. But I (and a majority of the council) think a policy of modest annual tax increases is a better way to deal with the problem than over reliance on surplus. We will use our 2002 year-end surplus of approximately $5,880,000 over a number of years to keep tax increases for municipal purposes on a reasonable upward incline, while gradually reducing the surplus. That way, everyone is made aware of the increasing costs of operating municipal government. And we don't delude ourselves that there is some magic formula known only to the Ramsey governing body allowing us to maintain a flat tax rate in the face of rising expenditures.

The reason why our taxes will go up is simple. Our expenses are going up (they go up every year), but our base of tax ratables is not expanding at a commensurate pace. On the revenue side, we are about 99% developed and cannot expect much in the way of new ratables to lessen the burden for those of us already here. State aid has been flat for the past two years. Given the state's fiscal crisis, we cannot expect more help from that quarter. Other factors impact on our revenue. With lower interest rates being a by-product of the poor economy, we will earn less income from surplus funds on deposit. We are seeing a reduction in governmental grants for necessary municipal services, like recycling.

On the appropriations (expense) side of the budget, costs of health insurance benefits for our employees are continuing their upward spiral. They are increasing $200,000 again this year, making this the 3rd year in a row of 20% increases. We have to pay for the property revaluation ordered by the county, and that will cost us $85,000 per year for the next five years. The state pension fund losses on the stock market will mean that we must pay out an estimated $500,000 in pension contributions for our employees in the next three years. In contrast, our pension contributions over the past three years have been negligible. Then, of course, you have this past winter's snow removal costs of approximately $85,000 in overtime and extra materials. We've applied for a grant, but must provide for that cost in our budget nonetheless.

That is not to say that we should throw our hands up in surrender. No one on your governing body advocates that approach. We are constantly looking for ways to economize and to minimize the impact on our citizens. We cut $235,000 in the legal expense line item in this year's budget, for example. Our borough administrator, negotiated a long-term garbage collection contract that will lock in this vital service at a very advantageous rate. We are also insisting on health insurance "give-backs" from our employees. We cannot continue to give free health benefits to every full time employee, including family coverage when applicable, without getting something in return. Unless we take action now when union contracts are up for renegotiation, we will lose control over that issue for the next three or four years.

We are also taking a strong stance on salary and wage increases. When inflation and the cost of living have been averaging less that 2% over the past five years, we can no longer justify giving employees salary increases in the 4 to 5% range. We want our employees to earn a fair living, but we cannot overpay them. If individual employees are not being fairly compensated for one reason or another, perhaps some adjustments are necessary on a case by case basis. But beyond those adjustments, we need to be firm.

We took other measures to keep taxes in check. For example, we moved $675,000 in Northwest Bergen Sewer Authority charges from the municipal budget to the public utility budget. (The public utility budget is part of the information available to you on-line and at the library.) That's where those charges should have been in the first place—they are an operating expense of the utility, not the municipality. The utility will be raising water and sewer fees for the first time in five years, but that is a prudent move in any event. The members of the Board of Public Works unanimously agreed with that policy decision. Their expenses have been going up, too, and revenue, because of the recent drought, has been dropping. Have any other utilities serving your home had a zero rate increase for the last five years? Of course not, and it is unreasonable to expect that the Ramsey water and sewer utility can operate any differently. (Incidentally, the Board of Public Works will be instituting a discount program for seniors and the disabled. Look for a letter explaining that in the next month or two.)

Another approach we will be taking is to rely less on the "pay as you go" philosophy and more on the "pay as you use" philosophy. In prior years, the governing body felt it was important to pay cash for all capital projects. If we needed a new fire truck, we paid $500,000 or so in cash for it. A new rescue squad truck? $260,000 in cash. New drainage projects or water main construction? Cash.

That approach has appeal, at first glance. We operate without debt and save interest charges. But why, one might ask, should a senior citizen in his or her 70's or 80's be paying in today's tax dollars for a benefit that Ramsey residents will enjoy for the next 20 or 30 or 40 years? A fire truck, for example, has a 20-25 year useful life. Why not stretch out payment over 15 or 20 years, so that people receiving the benefit are the ones who pay for it—not just the people who happen to be around today when we purchase it. Newly constructed water mains last for 50 years. Should a family whose breadwinner might be transferred in a few years be forced to pay in full for an improvement that will last half a century?

I think most economists and business experts would recommend bonding for long-term capital projects, especially with interest rates so low. That way, we lessen the impact on our current budget by spreading payments over a period that more closely resembles the useful life of the project. It is also a fairer approach. Yes, it will cost us interest, but the resulting lower current tax rate offsets that. Money has a time value.

We will continue to pay for less expensive items out of our

operating budget. For example, we have programmed $230,000 into this year's budget for road resurfacing and sidewalk repairs. We also have $1,100,000 set aside for other capital projects we may want to pay cash for. I propose taking this prudent, middle of the road course. I think a majority of the governing body will agree that such an approach serves the best interests of residents.

The pie chart comparisons in the budget mailer show how your property tax dollars are distributed. As you can see from the chart, the most significant portion of your tax dollar (67.9%) goes to support our outstanding school system. In many ways, the quality of our school system is responsible for the high property values we enjoy in Ramsey. The school budget is under the control of the Board of Education and only comes before the mayor and council in the event of a school budget defeat at the polls. Voting on this year's school budget is scheduled for April 15th. Last year, just 12% of the electorate bothered to vote on the school budget. That poor turnout is a disgrace, especially when one considers the implications involved. We should not allow our future to be decided by so few of us. I urge you to participate in this year's school budget decision and in the election of school board members. Let's strive for at least 50% voter participation.

Chapter 12

One achievement I'm particularly proud of was bringing Ramsey its first community band in 50 years. I had hired the "Ramapo" Wind Symphony to play at my swearing-in ceremony. Afterward, I had the idea of having the band change its name to the Ramsey Wind Symphony. I spoke with its director and founder, Peter Del Vecchio, a Ramsey resident, and he liked the idea. I proposed, subject to council approval, that the Borough would give the band $10,000 in annual support to cover its expenses. In exchange, the band would base itself in Ramsey and perform free concerts for residents throughout the year. The council supported me, and Ramsey had its own community band again.

A $10,000 expense, in the context of an $18 million dollar municipal budget, is not a big deal. Nevertheless, a group of Ramsey residents were incensed that I would "waste" taxpayers' money this way. They viewed the new band as an affront to the high school band. They were also mad about a whole lot of things and wrote an "Open Letter to Mayor Muti" to let me know of their displeasure in my performance as mayor, just a few months into my term. I include the letter here in its entirety to show an inevitable fact of politics: one man's eloquent expositor of truth, honor, and justice is another man's troublemaking gasbag.

"Dear Mr. Mayor,

As you approach your first hundred days in office, some concerned citizens feel the need to give you feedback. This letter would probably be best stated to you in private; however you are the one who feels the need to use the media to communicate all of your thoughts and whims to the public, so it is through a public forum that our thoughts are communicated back to you. The other reason for using a public medium is that while your election promise stated that you would be available to listen to the "voice of the people" and represent them, your replies to e-mails that express a difference of opinion about your position dismisses those concerns with a simple, "I disagree". We have no political agenda here. This is being written by some citizens who have become alarmed by your methodology.

Mr. Mayor, in the few months of your campaign and time in office you have done more to create a feeling of divisiveness and distrust than has existed in the town of Ramsey over the past twenty years. You publicly force your views onto issues in a way that shows total disregard to civility. Rather than promote cohesiveness, you seem to want to create controversy where there should be none by staking out your personal position in the media. Ramsey has various public committees whose appointees learn to become proficient in their special fields and exercise sound judgment. Why do you feel the need to inject your opinion? You do not carry a vote in the town council except in the case of a tie. Yet you seem to feel the need to influence any and all opinions prior to those times when your vote may be needed.

This is a very small community. We know each other. Our children have gone through the school system together. And we talk to each other. So when you try to force your hand behind the scenes, it becomes public knowledge very quickly. You recently authorized $10,000 paid to a musical group, the Ramapo Wind Ensemble [sic], to change their home and name to include Ramsey. While promoting the Arts within our community can not (and should not) be argued, the idea of paying any money at all for this particular purpose is heinous. These are local amateurs and volunteers. Offering them a home and a venue to promote their art should (and would) have been enough support. You publicly write about being a watch-dog over our dollars and then pay unnecessary sums to a group that happens to be led by a very vocal supporter of yours. In addition, the town of Ramsey has award-winning musical groups at the high school. They include the Marching Band, Jazz Band, Orchestra, and various Vocal groups. They would make fine representatives at any town function with no additional cost. Rather than criticizing the public schools, have you even thought about lending them your enthusiasm and support?

While on the subject of schools, you have taken a public stance questioning the validity of the pending school budget and potential plan to build a new Dater school. First of all, Ramsey has elected officials who are empowered to deal with these issues. Secondly, you have done a magnificent job of speaking out of both sides of your mouth depending on your audience. You have told parents of school children that you personally can vote for the budget, yet you state that as Mayor, you will not support the budget. Which constituency are you trying to appease? While it is in this community's best interests to have a school budget approved, you are expected to cast a decision should the budget ever be defeated. How can we trust you to cast an impartial vote in the best interests of the town when you have gone on record with a political/ personal agenda? As very ably explained by Superintendent DeYoung in the community meetings, the Board of Education has done an admirable job of containing costs to the regular operating school budget for many years. The current cost issues stem almost entirely from increases that are forced upon our budget by the State and Federal mandates, yet are not funded by them. Instead of creating factionalism within our town, would it not serve everyone's interests to work *with* the School Board to pass a budget that can accommodate our needs?

The referendum concerning Dater School has not even been placed into the public arena; however, you are already trying to sway opinion. You have criticized the School Board's use of a consultant, yet want to hire a consultant of your choosing. Why? Are you a better expert in consultants? Moreover, those of us who have lived here for a while and have had children attend Dater school know very well that this building was antiquated many decades ago, which was confirmed by the study. The Board of Education is elected to do their job. Why do you feel the need to exercise the Mayoral bully-pulpit to politicize this issue?

You have injected your opinion into police personnel issues, have attended PTO meetings to promote your opinions, and placed yourself into a self-proclaimed role of trying to micro-manage practically every organization in our community. While you may have been born in Ramsey, you have not lived in this town long enough, nor have you had enough personal experience to even have an opinion on all that takes place in the various organizations within this town. This is Ramsey, not 'Muti-town' and we are asking you to perform your duty as mayor—not to create your private fiefdom. In short, while you are certainly entitled to your opinion, both as an individual and as mayor, you seem to feel the need to create controversy over any issue so that you can 'weigh-in' and have your voice heard. This is not what you were elected to do and many people are becoming upset with your intrusive and 'over-the-top' methodology. As stated at the beginning of this letter, you have injected a lack of civility into the workings of this community by promoting divisiveness. You have professed to have good executive and administrative abilities. If you do, in fact, possess those skills Mr. Mayor, then use them to do your job—and nothing more."

I met with representatives of the group, but made little headway with them—not surprising, after their assertion, "This is Ramsey, not Muti-town." Several of these folks would remain my bitter political opponents throughout my tenure as mayor, joining a short-lived "Recall Mayor Muti" movement the following year. Needless to say, I did not heed their advice to refrain from "injecting my opinion into matters that didn't concern me."

The Ramsey Wind Symphony became one of the most popular activities in the Borough. I asked the band to perform an Independence Day Patriotic Concert—something that had been missing in Ramsey for at least half a century. Each year during my tenure as mayor, 5,000 or more residents turned out to listen to Sousa marches and thrill at the fireworks display. The band played at Ramsey Day, an annual celebration of our community spirit, and thousands attended those concerts, too. After I left office, the next administration continued this tradition, and continued its support of the Ramsey Wind Symphony.

The following article appeared as my "In the Arena" column of April 30, 2003.

Ars Gratia Artis

As a kid in the late 1940's and early 1950's, I often spent a rainy Saturday afternoon at the Ramsey Theater. For a quarter, you could see three or four cartoons, an episode of the latest serial, and a double feature. If one of the movies was a Metro-Goldwyn-Mayer production, it would start off with a roaring lion and this Latin motto: *Ars Gratia Artis*. I can't say that I knew what it meant back then, but three years of Latin under Miss Priesche at Ramsey High School enlightened me. "Art for the sake of art."

I'll concede that Alan Ladd outdrawing Jack Palance to save a bunch of sodbusters (*Shane*) wasn't exactly the highest form of art. But it did serve as a starting point for me, at least, and I've moved on to more challenging cultural experiences.

I guess that's why I was saddened when I read in *The Record* two weeks ago that the John Harms Center for the Arts in Englewood was closing down. It was a convenient place to see almost-Broadway quality productions without the expense and hassle of *schlepping* into the City. The John Harms theater was the local venue for Willie Nelson, among others, and I dragged my wife there two years running to see and hear Willie admonish all the mamas in the audience not to let their babies "grow up to be cowboys." (Okay, so maybe my artistic tastes haven't ascended as high as I let on.)

As a community, we should embrace opportunities to culturally enrich our lives and the lives of our children, don't you think? When Governor McGreevey proposed a cut in state support for the Arts as a budget-balancing measure this year, negative public reaction forced his retreat. Even in the face of a belt-tightening economy, we recognize the need for something more in our lives than bare necessities—something to inspire the heroic side of our nature. Wordsworth put it this way:

> *High is our calling, friend! Creative Art*
> *(Whether the instrument of words she use,*
> *Or pencil pregnant with ethereal hues),*
> *Demands the service of a mind and heart,*
> *Though sensitive, yet, in their weakest part,*

Heroically fashioned.

With that motive in mind, I recommended and the governing body approved an attempt to resurrect the Fine Arts Council, which had succumbed under the prior administration to poorly attended events and, I think, disillusionment among its members. A few years back, the FAC spent $2,500 to bring a Gilbert and Sullivan production to town. Eight people showed up for the performance. I can only assume the event was not promoted well—we are not a community of philistines, after all. I think we can do better.

At the reorganization meeting last January, I appointed and the council confirmed seven strong members to a newly constituted Fine Arts Council. The FAC is actively seeking residents who would like to serve on its Advisory Committee and help develop programs not just in music, but also in painting and other fine arts, photography, crafts, and performing arts.

The governing body also approved a $20,000 budget for the FAC in 2003 as a pledge of our support for the Arts in Ramsey. That doesn't necessarily mean the full amount will be spent; the FAC will recruit corporate sponsors and other patrons, which may lessen the need for tax dollars. We'll see how it goes.

If the FAC's first event is any barometer, they are off to a good start. On April 13th, despite beckoning spring weather and the Palm Sunday holiday, almost 150 people attended the Young People's Concert at Smith School, jointly sponsored by the FAC and the Ramsey Wind Symphony.

It was a magnificent event, reminiscent of Leonard Bernstein's concerts for young audiences. Peter Del Vecchio, conductor of the Ramsey Wind Symphony, created a program that enthralled young and old, alike. With each piece, we gained an appreciation for a new aspect of musical knowledge. But the learning was subtle, never overshadowing the music, which ranged from "Colonel Bogey's March" to the "William Tell Overture." The joy in the faces of young Melanie, as she sat listening with her dad, and young Nick, as he sat listening with his mom, was reflective of the experience of every kid in the audience. Maestro Del Vecchio auctioned off his baton and a chance to lead the band, with proceeds going toward a scholarship for a graduating member of the Ramsey High School Band. Nick's mom was high bidder, and he got to lead the band in a rousing rendition of "Stars and Stripes Forever." All children in the audience were invited to stand among the band members for the final number, there to experience not just the sound, but also the resonance of the music.

The Ramsey Wind Symphony was formerly known as the Ramapo Wind Symphony, a group with a long history of serving Ramsey, Mahwah, and Suffern. They've played at Ramsey Day for a decade and have offered neighborhood and Finch Park concerts in Ramsey, including a performance at the 9/11 Memorial last September. Funding for the group has been sporadic, with Mahwah's annual contribution and concert fees providing the bulk of its financing.

After the Ramapo Wind Symphony's performance at our reorganization meeting in January—enthusiastically applauded by 900+ residents in attendance—I came up with the idea of transforming the group into Ramsey's own community band. The borough council unanimously approved the move and agreed to provide a $10,000 budget in support. Residents who wish to become members of the band are invited to audition.

The cost to the average property owner to support the Ramsey Wind Symphony for the entire year is about $1.88. I'm not a smoker, but I think we can afford a community band for less than half the cost of a pack of cigarettes. The Ramsey Wind Symphony will be performing at least six concerts this year, including a major concert in June and a glorious Fourth of July weekend spectacular of patriotic tunes, complete with fireworks. As a boy, it cost me a quarter for an afternoon at the Ramsey Theater. Half a century later, I guess 31 cents per concert is a pretty good entertainment value for the entire family.

Chapter 13

From my "In the Arena" column of March 26, 2003. You can see why those "Open Letter to Mayor Muti" folks were so mad.

Karnak the Magnificent

Remember Johnny Carson, the pre-Leno host of NBC's "Tonight Show"? One of Carson's most popular comedy sketches was Karnak the Magnificent, all-knowing seer from the mystic East, who could put a sealed envelope to his turbaned head and divine the question contained therein. He would recite the answer, tear open the envelope with a flourish, and reveal the question—to the amazement of all.

Although I don't claim the powers of Karnak, I will give it a try. Ed McMahon is here with me now as I write this column; he is handing me a sealed envelope, and I am holding it to my head. Instead of a turban, I am wearing my old Brooklyn Dodgers cap. Wait a minute—I'm beginning to feel the answer forming in my brain. Yes, I have it!

> *Answer*: "Worse, worser, worsest."

I am tearing open the envelope and retrieving the slip of paper inside. Here is the question.

> *Question*: "Describe Ramsey's school budget for the next three years if the Board of Education fails to address the problems we face."

Yes, I know. This is no laughing matter, and I am not laughing. I am dead serious when I say to friends and political foes alike:

we'd better do something right now, or we are destined to reap a bitter harvest.

Already, I have committed a cardinal sin, a heinous crime in the minds of many constituents. I have had the audacity to question the way we spend our education dollars. In recent weeks, you have read articles and have seen a full-page ad in which I asked questions. Questions about the $26.5 million school facilities proposal of the Board of Education; questions about salary and health benefits we provide to teachers. The e-mail responses I have received to date have been mostly negative and part of an organized campaign—indicative, I think, of what will befall anyone who confronts this issue. Education is Ramsey's sacred cow.

If you have read this far and are upset with me, I beg you to suspend your outrage for just a few moments and hear me out. Give me an honest chance to make my case.

There are two separate matters to be considered. The first is this year's school budget, which will go before voters on April 15th; the second is the school facilities bond referendum, which is expected to be ready for a September vote. I will discuss only the school budget in this column, but will have much to say in coming months about the school facilities bond referendum.

With regard to the school budget, I attended all of the Superintendent's presentations to the various PTO's this month. I intend to vote *Yes* on the school budget in April, but will cast my affirmative vote with apprehension. I will vote *Yes* because the Board of Education (BOE) has done the best it could this year. I understand the BOE's frustration with the failure of our state and federal representatives to provide reasonable funding for the educational mandates they impose on us. State legislators do not have the political courage to create a broad-based tax program to support education and give property tax relief. Congress enacted the Individuals with Disabilities Education Act (I.D.E.A.) in 1975 and promised to provide 40% of the funding necessary to implement it. For the first twenty years or so, the Feds funded less than 9% of the costs, on average. In the last two or three years, federal funding has crept up to about 17%, far short of promised support. Considered an affluent school district, Ramsey still gets less than 6% of its I.D.E.A. costs funded.

In the years ahead, the picture only gets bleaker. It would be irresponsible of us to wait for others to solve our problems.

Having said all that in support of this year's school budget, let me tell you why I have a sense of foreboding about the future. In his budget presentations, the Superintendent attributed most of the problems we face to special education costs. It is a sensitive subject, and I think the Superintendent handled it well. But he failed to give the same degree of emphasis to an integral part of the problem: labor costs and employee benefits.

Health insurance premiums have increased about 20% a year for the last three years, with no relief in sight. We provide this benefit free to Ramsey teachers and include free family coverage for tenured teachers. The cost in 2002-2003 ranges between $4,200 and $4,700 for a single teacher, $6,400 and $9,600 for a husband and wife, and $11,000 and $12,000 for the family plan. That's a wonderful benefit, and perhaps it was justified years ago when teachers were underpaid and health insurance costs were more reasonable. But teachers are no longer underpaid. They make a very good living, with an excellent retirement plan. Under the current contract, a top step teacher earns up to $87,000 for about 190 workdays per year. Over 28% of Ramsey teachers earn more than $80,000. Not bad.

Newly hired teachers earn less, of course. The Ramsey school system currently employs over 100 untenured teachers, and they get free single health benefits only. (A teacher must serve three years and a day to become tenured.) Tenure, for all intents and purposes, means a guaranteed job for life. It also means, in Ramsey, free family plan health insurance, at more than twice the cost to taxpayers. Perhaps we can afford to keep giving free health insurance benefits this year or next; but unless we do something to bring insurance costs under control, we will be buried by them.

Take a look at the budget flyer the BOE mailed to every household last week. The employee benefits line item is $3,436,058 for school year 2002-2003. That same line item in the proposed budget for 2003-2004 jumps to $4,645,734, a 35% increase. The major part of the benefit cost is health insurance, but it also includes pension contributions. In three years, assuming a more conservative 25% annual increase, the cost of health insurance and other benefits for our school employees will almost double, to $9,073,699.

Salary and benefits for all school employees make up 65% of the entire school budget. It is the most controllable aspect of the budget. So why aren't we controlling it?

Right now, we have a window of opportunity to do something, a window that will soon close and will remain closed for three or four years. The Board of Education is in the midst of negotiations with the teachers' union for a new contract. The corporate world is requiring employees to share this health insurance burden, as is every other sector of our economy. Why should teachers be exempt?

I am not suggesting a major giveback. If we were to require just a $50 per week contribution from each employee, that would amount to $2,000 over the 40-week school year. That's not too much to ask of teachers in exchange for a $12,000 benefit. The charge could be structured as a percentage of salary, so that teachers earning more pay more and teachers at the lower end of the salary scale pay less. The total annual savings to the school district (and to taxpayers) would be about $800,000 if this concept were to be applied to all employees. That's almost half of the projected tax increase in the new budget.

We also have to resist the practice of giving 4 or 5% annual salary increases to government employees when the cost of living (inflation) has averaged under 2% for the past five years.

Our BOE is no different from those of neighboring towns. It is reluctant to take on the powerful teachers' union. The Ridgewood BOE recently signed a multi-year deal with its teachers, granting annual 4.5% salary increases without getting one dollar of health insurance givebacks in return. According to newspaper reports, Ridgewood teachers had engaged in a number of sordid job actions to put the pressure on, and their strategy worked. The BOE caved in, and Ridgewood taxpayers will pay the price. Those folks can afford it; many Ramsey residents cannot.

Chapter 14

Shipmates Stand Together

"In the Arena," April 9, 2003.

A few years ago, the author of a best-selling work of non-fiction claimed that everything he needed to know, he learned in kindergarten. I don't think I'd go that far, but I often rely, forty years later, on principles that were instilled at the U.S. Naval Academy.

One such principle was the idea of "shipmates," a feeling of camaraderie that often develops in a group facing hardship together—a willingness to go the extra mile for one of your own. Shakespeare's Henry V, addressing his troops on St. Crispin's Day, put it this way.

And Crispin shall ne'er go by,
From this day to the ending of the world,
But we in it shall be remembered;
We few, we happy few, we band of brothers.

Today, King Henry would have to adjust his thinking ("we band of brothers and sisters") in recognition of the courage and professionalism of women in our Armed Forces.

At Annapolis, we had a fight song most often heard at football games, but we knew it translated to a larger context.

Shipmates stand together,
Don't give up the ship.
Fair or stormy weather,
We won't give up,
won't give up,
the ship.

It is a wonderful concept and is already at work in our community. Ramsey police and volunteers in the emergency services practice it every day—men and women, standing shoulder to shoulder, putting themselves at risk for our benefit. Hundreds of residents display the same trait in smaller, but equally important ways: working behind the scenes to help those in need or, simply, to make Ramsey a better place to live.

Perhaps we can do more. Here are a few of my thoughts, but I welcome any suggestions you may have.

At the last meeting of the governing body, the borough council unanimously approved the creation of a new volunteer position in Ramsey: human services coordinator. (I stress that it is a non-paid position, costing taxpayers little or nothing.)

The idea of a human services coordinator stemmed from a recent visit to the Center for Food Action (CFA) in Mahwah. Public Advocate Harris Recht and Gina Ratto, wife of Councilman Joe Ratto, accompanied me. We were briefed by CFA director Bea O'Rourke on her organization's activities. Mainly, CFA provides food to needy families in northwest Bergen County and parts of Passaic County. But here's the shocker. The town with the second highest number of CFA clients is Ramsey. (Mahwah has the most.) Over one hundred Ramsey families routinely seek food and other emergency assistance from the CFA because they can't manage alone.

Bea was full of praise for help she receives from Ramsey churches, scouts, and the high school student council; but she was especially thankful for the outstanding work of students at the Eric Smith School, under the leadership of its principal, Dr. Richard Wiener. Smith School students recently marked their eighth year of service to the CFA.

Despite all the help from various groups in Ramsey, Bea suggested that local government could do more. She asked if I would participate in this year's CROP Walk for Hunger in October, and I readily agreed. More important, she recommended that we find someone to coordinate services for Ramsey's needy. A person who could act as a resource center and direct people to the services they require, whether it be Meals on Wheels for homebound elderly, Shelter Our Sisters for abused women, or, for that matter, the Center for Food Action for the hungry. It would require a special person,

Bea said, someone who would be willing to spend weeks learning the ropes and many hours each week putting needy families in touch with the right agency. Someone who would be tough enough to deal with the emotional demands of the position.

That's when Gina Ratto said, "I'll do it."

On March 26, 2003, I appointed Gina Ratto as Ramsey's first human services coordinator. She has already begun her training program and will, I predict, serve Ramsey with distinction.

One of the functions I envision for this position is not only directing people to outside agencies for assistance, but also establishing a corps of Ramsey residents willing to render assistance themselves, a band of brothers and sisters who will answer the call when help is needed. For example, many elderly and disabled residents found great difficulty dealing with all the snow this winter. Sidewalks had to be shoveled so children could safely walk to school, but some residents just couldn't cope. Next winter, I think we can maintain a list of able-bodied men and women who will lend a hand to such folks. If not to shovel a sidewalk, perhaps to provide a ride to a doctor's office. Or simply, to pay a visit to a lonely old-timer.

Let's stand up and be counted when our shipmates are in need.

Chapter 15

A Run for the New Jersey State Senate

My decision in April 2003 to run for state senate against an entrenched, well-financed incumbent in a heavily Republican district, after serving just three months, as mayor was the worst political decision of my brief public career. And the costliest. (See Chapter 16, "Writing My Political Obituary.")

First, I hadn't proven myself to my core constituency, the people of Ramsey. Ramsey was the third largest community in the 39th Legislative District, and to have a prayer of winning the senate race, I had to do even better than the 62% vote I received just five months earlier. Although I would have continued on as mayor, still devoting 40 hours a week or more to my hometown, people didn't understand that. They thought I was bailing out on them, before promises were kept. Both the mayor's job and the state senator's job are part-time, and practically all municipal elected officials and state legislators have full-time jobs to earn their livelihood.

Second, I knew I wouldn't get much, if any, campaign funding from either the Democratic County Organization (they hadn't supplied more than token support in my run for mayor) or the State Democratic Committee. Both organizations wrote off my chances of winning, and it turns out they were right.

Third, the incumbent had been around for 22 years, had great name recognition in the district, and had big corporate donors falling all over themselves to get on his bandwagon.

But my opponent did have some negatives. Here's what The Star-Ledger said about him on May 11, 2003:

"Sen. Gerald Cardinale, the blunt conservative from Bergen County, told an audience last week that money can indeed buy votes. He was speaking at the New Jersey Medical Society's annual convention.... As is his habit, Cardinale let his audience have it between the eyes. If New Jersey doctors each gave $500, he said, 'Legislators would trip over themselves to support your cause.' Putting theory to practice, Cardinale then introduced his wife in the back row, and invited doctors to buy tickets [at $500 each] to his upcoming golf outing."

Cardinale had been cited by newspapers on several occasions as the senator taking the most in corporate gifts. He was chairman of the Senate Commerce Committee when Republicans controlled the Senate, and got an all-expenses paid vacation to warmer climes every winter, compliments of the banking industry. In my mind, this guy had vulnerability. All I had to do was communicate the facts to the public, and they would support me in droves.

I managed to raise some funds, mostly in small contributions from individuals, but the bulk of my funding came from my own resources. Actually, I went into hock, borrowing heavily—loans that had to be converted into a second mortgage I'll be paying off the rest of my life—to buy newspaper space and send mailers out. I knew I could write dynamite ads and mail pieces—the fact-filled kind I had used successfully in my mayoral campaign, properly sourced and presented in a straightforward way the public would get. I didn't mind the debt. It would be worth it, I thought, just to have a chance to change things in Trenton. It was the old "truth and justice" mentality from my prosecutor days: how can the good guy not prevail?

My campaign was bolstered when The Record gave me its endorsement and urged voters to elect me for a change.

As Election Day neared, I was filled with hope. I ignored the slick, negative mailers my opponent was sending out every other day. They were filled with trash—half-truths and outright falsehoods the public would see through. One flyer pictured me as a cartoon Pinocchio and called me a liar for running out on the people of Ramsey before I finished my term.

I had taken the high road in my campaign. Sure I attacked my opponent's record, but with citations to the source of every fact I asserted, including state campaign disclosure records and legislative voting records. For example, I pointed out instances where my opponent took money from an organization and shortly thereafter, introduced legislation to benefit that organization.

Here are two of my campaign pieces from the 2003 State Senate race. The first is an ad I ran at the start of my campaign; the second is a mailer I sent out in mid-September to every Independent voter in the 39th District.

Telling the Hard, Honest Truth

I'm new at politics, so forgive me if I take a novel approach to communicating with the public. I believe elected officials should be honest and straightforward, even when their message may not be to the public's liking. The unpleasant truth? *New Jersey is in the midst of its most severe fiscal crisis since the Great Depression.*

In his first two years in office, Governor McGreevey has had to deal with $14 billion in budget deficits. The budget this year was balanced with the help of, among other things, a one-time advance of $1.6 billion in tobacco litigation settlement money. Next year, that Band-Aid will not be available, and we face another $4-5 billion deficit. That means less property tax relief, less aid to municipalities, less aid to schools.

We cannot expect any help from the federal government. Just weeks ago, President Bush announced that it will take another $87 billion to pacify and rebuild Iraq, not counting the $79 billion already spent. This comes on top of record federal deficits, a seemingly untouchable tax cut program (no matter what new calamity strikes us) that will reduce federal revenue by hundreds of billions more in the next decade, and a war on terrorism that presents the most frightening and costly specter of all. The Department of Homeland Security has said another terrorist attack on the United States is likely. God forbid it should ever come, but imagine what new havoc it will wreak on our economy, the already high unemployment rate, the stock market, and people's life savings.

According to *The New York Times*, the cumulative federal deficit will, over the next eight years, reach $2.3 trillion. Yes, trillion. We don't have the money, of course, so it will have to be borrowed, causing interest rates to soar and further complicating any hope for a quick economic recovery. Who will pay the bill? Our children and our children's children.

Any politician who tells you he will meet this challenge by eliminating waste in the budget or by firing all the lawyers is feeding you pabulum and insulting your intelligence. Of course we must eliminate waste wherever it is found. Of course we must get rid of the patronage jobs our system of campaign finance seems to perpetuate, no matter which party is in power. But those measures, alone, will not close a $5 billion budget gap next year. They won't even come close.

I don't pretend to have all the answers, but I do know this. Unless leaders of both parties come together, with a minimum of partisan bickering and political posturing, and make an honest effort to solve this problem, we may, indeed, see Great Depression II in the not too distant future. What is required is statesmanship, not one-upmanship.

**Richard Muti, an independent Democrat—
beholden to no one, promised to no one,
owned by no one.**

- 1964 graduate of the United States Naval Academy
- Navy pilot, 1964 – 1969; plane commander of P-3 Orion
- 1971 graduate of Harvard Business School
- 1980 graduate of Rutgers Law School
- Served 19 years as a prosecutor, rising to deputy first assistant prosecutor in Bergen County. Fired in August 2000 for protesting wasteful $7,000,000 expenditure of public resources.
- Taught English at Rutgers and William Paterson Universities; taught politics and government, history, and criminal justice at Fairleigh Dickinson University.
- Elected mayor of Ramsey in November 2002 by largest margin in any contested election, defeating 4-term Republican incumbent by 1,350 votes.

Dear Independent Voter:

As a plebe at the Naval Academy many years ago, I "volunteered" for special duty. My roommates and I were shining shoes to get ready for inspection, when in walked a first classman. We sprang to attention, staring straight ahead while the omnipotent Firstie looked each of us over. Finally, he settled on me. Peering at my name tag, he said, "How much do you weigh, Mr. Muti."

"One hundred seventy pounds, Sir," I replied.

"Close enough," he said. "Report to the gym tomorrow at 1600 hours. We need a heavyweight." The Firstie was manager of the Fourth Battalion boxing team, and I'd just volunteered to get into a ring for the first time in my life, with bruisers about thirty pounds heavier than I.

My boxing career was mercifully brief—just that one season. I ended with a record of one win and four losses. My one win, I hasten to admit, was by forfeit. The guy in my weight class didn't show. One thing I'm proud of, though. I took lots of hits in my four bouts, but not one opponent knocked me down. At the end of each 3-round match, I was standing upright, my nose bleeding profusely, but on my feet.

I'm up against another heavyweight this November—Senator Gerald Cardinale. He has a huge campaign war chest, thanks to his cozy relationship with special interest groups. I fully expect he'll be flailing away at me soon, both above and below the belt. But come November 4th, I will still be standing. And I will be the choice of a majority of voters. Let me tell you why. We need new leadership in Trenton—**Leadership** *for a change*—and I have the training, experience, and commitment to bring about that change.

I am a graduate of the United States Naval Academy and served as a Navy pilot in the late 1960's. I left the service to accept a full-tuition scholarship to Harvard Business School. After earning my M.B.A. in 1971, I worked in real estate for five years before deciding to attend the night study program at Rutgers Law School in Newark. It wasn't easy—four nights a week for four years, while holding down a full-time job. I graduated in 1980 and became an attorney at the age of 40.

I went to work for the Bergen County Prosecutor and, in three years, prosecuted more than 30 jury trials, achieving a 95%

conviction rate. Later, I served as a municipal prosecutor. In eleven years, I prosecuted over 2,000 drunk driving cases (with a 99% conviction rate) and many other offenses. I also spoke to thousands of high school students about substance abuse and driving while under the influence. I think I made a difference in the life choices of some of those youngsters.

In 1995, after my youngest child completed college, I returned to the Bergen County Prosecutor's Office as chief administrator, in charge of an $18 million budget. But I was also assigned to prosecute significant cases, like police corruption, official misconduct, and murder. I was lead prosecutor in a Teaneck case you may remember reading about in the late 1990's—the murder of the Sealy Mattress Company heir and armed robbery of his 89-year old mother. Both killers were convicted and sent to prison for the rest of their lives.

In August 2000, my career as a prosecutor came to an abrupt end. You may also have read about it. I wrote to the Bergen County Executive to protest my boss's plan to spend $7,000,000 in public money to buy an office building, when less expensive alternatives existed. I also objected to overstaffing the BCPO at a time when the crime rate was decreasing. We were spending millions on extra personnel, when we should have been downsizing to save tax dollars. I was fired the same day I wrote my letter. (Visit my web site at www.mayormuti.com to read the letter that got me fired.)

It was my duty to care about how government spent your money. It's that same sense of duty that guides me as mayor of Ramsey and leads me to make this run for state senate.

In this traditionally Republican 39th district, you need to know that I am an *independent* Democrat—beholden to no one, promised to no one, owned by no one. I refuse to be placed into any ideological cubbyhole. Ramsey residents accepted my independent stance when, against all odds, they voted a 16-year incumbent out of office and elected me mayor. More than a quarter of the registered Republicans in Ramsey voted for me, as did most Democrats and Independents.

As mayor, I've appointed men and women to local boards and commissions without regard to party affiliation. Most residents in the 39th legislative district are not affiliated with either major party.

Which proves a point, I think. People do not like heavy-handed partisanship. It gets in the way of good government.

With a 4-2 split council, I've had to work with the Republican majority to get things done. Together, but on my initiative, we hired new legal counsel and saved taxpayers $100,000 in the first six months of 2003. We raised the municipal tax rate just 2%—less than the rate of inflation—but actually cut budgeted expenditures, despite Trenton's continued indifference to the plight of middle class property owners. With Republican support, I was able to put in place a prudent budget that will protect taxpayers. We will end this year with a $5 million surplus and be in a good position to meet the expected fiscal challenges next year.

Senator Cardinale has been around for 22 years. In some ways, he has done an adequate job, but in far too many *other* ways, he's been an abysmal failure—an embarrassment, in fact. You've undoubtedly read about him accepting gifts from the banking industry, which he regulates as chair of the Senate Commerce Committee. His blatant fund-raising activities, skirting the line between ethical and unethical, represent another lapse in judgment. In 1995, for example, the Joint Legislative Committee on Ethical Standards criticized Senator Cardinale for a letter his aide sent to chiropractors, a letter Cardinale knew about and condoned. Here's what one newspaper said: "Say you've got an important piece of legislation in Trenton, and you get a letter from an aide of the state senator who is blocking the legislation. The letter encourages you and your colleagues to contribute $135 apiece to meet the senator at a fund-raiser and try to change his mind. Does this sound like a shakedown to you?" Source: *The Record*, August 3, 1995.

The ethics panel said Senator Cardinale's "actions and inactions were unacceptable."

Our senator has taken large campaign contributions from special interest groups. When their interests collide with the public interest, where do you think Cardinale will stand? Go to the web site of the NJ Election Law Enforcement Commission and search required campaign filings Cardinale has made over the years. Large contributors are listed. Then go to the web site of the NJ State Legislature and search for bills Cardinale has proposed. Tie-ins to the money he has received are glaringly obvious. Cardinale opposes

limits on contributions from individuals, PACs, and corporations—
he takes thousands from people who want access and who get access
to the powerful chairman of the Senate Commerce Committee.

Apparently, they get their money's worth. Not only does the
senator promote the interests of his pay-to-play pals, he also votes
too frequently against the best interests of people in the 39th
legislative district. For example, he voted "no" on the Family Leave
Act, a bill protecting jobs of workers who take *unpaid* leave to care
for a newborn child or seriously ill family member. Happily, the
Senate passed the legislation overwhelmingly, and it is now the
law of this state. It is also the law of our nation, thanks to former
Congresswoman Marge Roukema, who championed the Family
Leave Act at the federal level.

Mr. Cardinale voted against requiring health insurers to
cover prostate cancer tests. He cast the only "no" vote on a bill to
require Lyme disease coverage. He voted against mental health
and infertility coverage. He has consistently voted against issues
of particular importance to women. For example, he cast the only
"no" vote on a bill extending unemployment benefits to victims of
domestic violence. He also cast the only "no" vote on a bill to clarify
procedures in civil actions alleging sexual abuse. Fortunately, 38
other senators from both parties voted "yes." He cast the only "no"
votes on bills to make it easier for the state to collect child support
payments from deadbeat dads. He voted "no" on a bill to increase
penalties for consumer fraud and "no" on a bill to protect seniors
and disabled citizens against eviction.

When you talk to friends about the campaign and vote on
November 4th, keep in mind my background, independence, and
commitment to represent you well.

Sincerely,

Richard Muti

Chapter 16

In April 2003, just months into my term as mayor, I announced my candidacy for New Jersey State Senate. As stated earlier, it was a mistake—not the desire to bring about desperately needed change in the state capital, but the timing of that effort. New Jersey law permitted service as both a mayor and state legislator, both offices being part-time, and I fully intended, if elected, to serve out my term as mayor. That was my priority. But I had not yet proven myself to the people of Ramsey, and it appeared, with help from my political opponents, as though I was abandoning them. I hadn't yet brought about changes I had promised, although I knew those would come in due course. Although polling more votes than any Democrat had ever done in the district, I took a drubbing from the incumbent, who many believed was one of the worst legislators in office. He was a Republican in a heavily Republican district, and I guess that is what mattered most to the electorate. Winning that race was a long shot at best, but I plunged into it with all the idealism I could summon.

Losing the district vote was expected, but I did not expect that I would lose my hometown. These were the folks who had elected me mayor a year before by landslide proportions. In the state senate race, they went against me, two to one. It broke my heart, and in the aftermath, filled with the sting of that overwhelming rejection by my own hometown, I wrote the following article as an "In the Arena" column on November 12, 2003. Another mistake. I should have kept my mouth shut and my feelings to myself.

My article became another plank in the "Recall Mayor Muti" petition drive in 2004. That movement, led by former supporters, fizzled out soon after it began, but it did cause me embarrassment, a desired effect by its proponents, I suppose. It also made me a better mayor, I think. Was it Nietzsche who said, "What does not kill you makes you stronger"?

Writing My Political Obituary

My first inclination after votes were counted on election night was to call it quits. I've always admired the British tradition that requires leaders to resign when faced with a vote of "no confidence" in Parliament. I half-expected to lose my senate race in the 39th; it is, indeed, a safe Republican district, as I learned at great personal cost. Sen. Cardinale is a formidable candidate, with unlimited resources and few scruples in using those resources. What was unexpected, however, was the extent of anti-Muti fervor here in Ramsey. To lose my hometown by a two to one margin was "the unkindest cut of all" and a resounding vote of *no confidence* from my own constituents.

A friend pointed out that Cardinale received no more votes than my opponent in the mayoral election last year and that his vote total, therefore, could be considered a base vote of those who have always been opposed to my reform measures. Perhaps that is true, but I will adopt the more pessimistic interpretation. My failure to inspire those in favor of my program to vote is also, in my mind, a vote of no confidence. It brings to an end my brief political career, but I shall strive to be a productive mayor for the remaining three years of my term. Then, I shall retire from public life. I'll complete my term because there is still much to be done. Here are just a few examples.

At our November 12th meeting at my urging, the council will introduce a "pay-to-play" ordinance. For those unfamiliar with state politics, *pay-to-play* is the practice whereby political contributors are rewarded with public contracts and jobs by politicians they supported. During our campaign last year, my running mates and I voluntarily limited contributions from anyone intending to do business with the Borough of Ramsey to $250, but we were under no legal requirement to do so. The corrupting influence of money is not so much evident here in Ramsey as it is at the county and state levels, where $40,000,000 was spent in this last election.

Unless there is a groundswell of public outrage over this practice, starting at the local level, I don't think legislators or governors will pay much attention. They stand to lose too much. That's why I'd like Ramsey to be in the forefront of reform. If we enact an ordinance and other communities in Bergen County follow suit, perhaps the county will take action. If Bergen enacts a law prohibiting the practice, perhaps state leaders will be influenced for the better.

Another long-standing practice in Ramsey that must be reformed is our policy of giving employees a "golden parachute" when they leave government employment. Here is how that little-known policy works. We give employees paid sick leave days, from 10 to 20 per year depending on what union or management level an employee is a member of. Employees are allowed to "bank" unused sick leave. That means it is carried forward to use in the future if a serious illness strikes the employee or a family member. That part is okay, but here is the troublesome part.

When an employee leaves government service in Ramsey, he or she is allowed to sell back to the Borough half of his or her unused sick leave days. Wait—it gets better. Sick leave days that were banked twenty years prior, when the employee was earning a lot less, are sold back to the Borough at the going rate of pay when the employee departs. Our former borough attorney, for example, in addition to receiving a quarter of a million a year for his last four years of employment, was presented with a check for $124,000 when he was removed by me last January. It was a little going away present from borough taxpayers, and there wasn't a thing I could do about it. I was also forced to keep him on for another year representing two boards, each of which meets once a month, at the rate of $3,500 a month to ease the pain of his departure, or else the council would not have allowed me to replace him. (The Republican council has controlled things for the past 20 years and still controls things now.) That albatross will be removed on December 31st, when I hope to further reduce legal expenses next year—beyond the $125,000 I saved us this year.

The Borough of Ramsey has an accumulated liability to its employees of over $1,000,000 in banked sick leave. Fortunately, the borough administrator has been providing in our budget for the transfer of $100,000 a year for the past few years to a dedicated account to pay out these future sums to departing employees. That will lessen the impact of several "golden parachutes" being handed out in one year.

In coming months I will propose that the council adopt an ordinance to reform this policy. I am in favor of employees being able to save sick leave for future needs—in the event of a catastrophic illness, for example—but I want to limit the buy-back amount for everyone. (A few unions have a limitation, but non-union personnel and police, who receive the highest salaries, do not.) I think a cap of $15,000 per departing employee is fair. We should also set a maximum of 15 sick leave days per year and enact a provision that sick leave days get banked at the rate of pay at which they were earned. In the recently concluded police contract, I was able to negotiate some relief for taxpayers by limiting buy-backs to the salary level of the rank at which the sick leave was earned. But that provision doesn't kick in until 2006. It is difficult to change police employment policies because of their right to binding arbitration. It is not difficult to change this policy for all other employees. All that is required is action by the council.

Some employees need salary adjustments. I don't think they're being fairly compensated for their duties and responsibilities. This is especially true among our lower paid employees, such as the clerical and office staff and library staff. As I continue to negotiate union contracts for lower paid employees, I will attempt to rectify these inequities. Any contract I negotiate is subject, of course, to council approval.

I have also been trying for months to get the council to look at inequities in base salary for certain management personnel. In June 2002, for example, a male assistant superintendent in the department of public works was hired at a base salary higher than that being paid to three female department heads with more job responsibilities and many more years of service. (The male employee is an excellent worker and I don't mean to disparage his worth. It is a matter of fairness, though.) After my prodding on this issue, the council agreed to hire a consultant to review job descriptions, responsibilities, and salaries of all non-union personnel and to make recommendations for fair and commensurate compensation. I think that is a good approach to the problem.

While I want to insure fair compensation for all employees, I'll continue to press for reductions in the cost of health insurance benefits. As previously noted, the police contract I negotiated will save $96,500 every year, beginning in 2004. I have proposals on the table with other unions to save at least $100,000 additional a year. Once again, those proposals will be subject to council approval. I will try to be fair with existing employees and soften the blow by increasing salaries a bit. I will also try to put into place for *newly hired* employees a requirement that they contribute to the cost of family health insurance benefits. Costs of health insurance are increasing 20% annually. With a current cost of $12,000 per employee for family coverage, we have no choice but to take action now if we want to be solvent ten years from now. The unions don't like it, and our employees don't like it. But as I think you've learned about me by now, I don't care about winning popularity contests (or elections, it seems).

Speaking of elections, let me state afterward, as I did before, that property taxes will continue to go up. Anyone who thinks otherwise is living in a dream world. The key is to keep increases at or near the rate of inflation, as we did in 2003 when the municipal government increase was set at 2%, or $40 for the average home.

Finally, let me say that I will continue to speak my mind for the remaining three years of my public service. For those who feel I lack diplomacy, I shall try to be more diplomatic. For those who think I am too controlling, I shall try to be less so. For those who want me to shut up . . . sorry, can't do that.

Chapter 17

One of the most satisfying aspects of being mayor was the "bully pulpit" it afforded, not just in my writings, but also in public addresses.

Memorial Day Address—May 31, 2004

Anyone who delivers a Memorial Day address must surely be overwhelmed by the task. How does one put into words the sentiments of a grateful nation? Can we ever adequately express what we owe to brave men and women killed or wounded in service to their country?

One person came closest, in a speech he gave on a warm autumn day in the middle of what had been a Pennsylvania cornfield. I refer, of course, to the speech President Abraham Lincoln gave on November 19, 1863, at the dedication of the Gettysburg National Cemetery.

There is much myth surrounding that speech, including the belief that Lincoln scribbled it on the back of an envelope while en route by train to Gettysburg. Years ago, I read historian Garry Wills' book on the subject. Wills was of the opinion that Lincoln had spent days crafting his masterpiece, writing draft after draft until he was satisfied.

Lincoln wasn't even the featured speaker at the Gettysburg dedication. That honor fell to Edward Everett, one of the most famous orators of the day, and Everett didn't disappoint. He delivered a two-hour stemwinder, filled with flowery language most Americans of the time equated with good oratory.

When Everett finished to tumultuous applause, Lincoln rose and walked to the podium.

Lincoln was not the most popular man in a nation grown weary with almost three years of civil war and heavy casualties. His political enemies had been hurling invective upon invective at him; the press portrayed him as a bumbling baboon. Now, we view him as savior of our nation, but back then, his legacy was much in doubt. At war's end, 617,000 men from North and South would lose their lives. Lincoln, himself, was convinced he would not win reelection. It was not until General Sherman won the battle of Atlanta in the fall of 1864 that Lincoln felt confident he would prevail and the Union would be preserved.

In this atmosphere of unrest, this political turmoil, this nation divided, Lincoln rose to speak. In the 271 words of his Gettysburg Address, Lincoln reminded his countrymen of principles perhaps forgotten in the heat of events at hand. He captured the essence of why we fight in defense of our country, why we honor those who fall, why we are Americans.

I can think of no more fitting way to reassert those principles we hold so dear than to repeat Lincoln's words:

"Four score and seven years ago our fathers brought forth on this continent, a new nation, conceived in Liberty, and dedicated to the proposition that all men are created equal. Now we are engaged in a great civil war, testing whether that nation, or any nation so conceived and so dedicated, can long endure. We are met on a great battlefield of that war. We have come to dedicate a portion of that field, as a final resting place for those who here gave their lives that that nation might live. It is altogether fitting and proper that we should do this. But, in a larger sense, we cannot dedicate – we cannot consecrate – we can not hallow – this ground. The brave men, living and dead, who struggled here, have consecrated it, far above our poor power to add or detract.

"The world will little note, nor long remember what we say here, but it can never forget what they did here. It is for us the living, rather, to be dedicated here to the unfinished work which they who fought here have thus far so nobly advanced. It is rather for us to be here dedicated to the great task remaining before us – that from these honored dead we take increased devotion to that cause for which they gave the last full measure of devotion – that we here highly resolve that these dead shall not have died in vain – that this nation, under God, shall have a new birth of freedom – and that government of the people, by the people, for the people, shall not perish from the earth."

Chapter 18

The War in Iraq

Initially, like most Americans, I accepted the President's assessment of the threat Iraq posed to our national security and even wrote an article urging my constituents to stand behind our leader, despite my misgivings about his failure to explore diplomatic solutions to the problem. But, as it became apparent that the case for war had been "cooked up," I began writing and speaking out against the Bush administration and its grossly incompetent and, in my mind, criminal handling of the Iraq crisis—a series of events that will be, I fear, the most devastating foreign policy blunder in our nation's history. Here are three pieces that express how I felt.

The Forbidden Image of this Memorial Day

"In the Arena," May 19, 2004

The circumstances in Iraq—over 750 dead, thousands more wounded—will be uppermost in our minds as we lay wreaths, say prayers, and remember this Memorial Day. Yet, a photograph that graphically but respectfully brought home the depth of our loss has become the forbidden image of the Iraq war.

A civilian contractor with the Air Force, involved with transporting bodies of American war dead to the air base in Dover, Delaware, photographed the coffins, row upon row, each draped with the flag. The Pentagon fired the contractor and her husband. Both had violated federal rules against photographing returning war dead—rules that probably had their origin in the Viet Nam war, when television coverage of returning body bags numbering in the thousands gave support to the anti-war movement.

Such images demean the dead, officials charged, and cause unnecessary pain and suffering to family members. But I don't buy it in this case. The government objected, I think, because the photos were a dramatic reminder of the costs of war and the consequences of poorly made decisions.

Readers of this column will recall that I accepted the Bush administration's warnings of an imminent threat to the United States and reluctantly supported the decision to go to war against Saddam Hussein's regime. (*Ramsey Suburban News*, March 5, 2003.) Here is what I said, in part:

"I support President Bush's handling of the Iraq crisis, although I would have preferred less saber-rattling and fewer avowals of 'time is running out.' We've drawn so many lines in the sand that our words are becoming meaningless. Secretary of State Colin Powell's diplomatic initiatives were undermined by more hawkish elements in the Bush administration. It now appears that war is all but inevitable."

Now, I think, it is abundantly clear that the compelling reasons President Bush, Vice President Cheney and others put forth to make their case for war simply didn't exist. It was a rush to judgment, influenced by preconceived notions and lousy intelligence. Sure, American and British forces (also known as "the Coalition") ousted a brutal dictator, but brutal dictators abound in this world. Now that weapons of mass destruction have not been found, deposing Saddam Hussein is put forth as sufficient justification, in and of itself, for the war. But that was not what they told us beforehand. Then, it was the looming threat to America that drove the war engine, that justified sending these kids, poorly equipped and under-manned, to fight. We were told the Iraqi people would welcome us as liberators, but daily television coverage of Iraqis dancing and shouting for joy at the death of yet another American show how wrong that assumption was. It was a grave miscalculation.

I have no doubt President Bush feels deeply for the families of those who have been killed or wounded. I am not a Bush basher, but any reasonable American must see that his policies have failed miserably. That is the truth of the matter and not political partisanship, of which I care little. His inattention to the consequences of our action in Iraq is glaringly apparent. And the news keeps getting worse. The prisoner abuse at Abu Ghraib may have irreparably damaged our ability to win the hearts and minds of the Iraqi people.

In the closing paragraph to my article last year, I said

"I hope President Bush sees us through this crisis with wisdom and courage. The brave young people we are about to send in harm's way must have a united home front. Let's get behind them and our president. I respect every American's right of free speech and assembly, but there comes a time to stand with our leaders against the enemy. That time is now."

Now, I'm not so sure we should stand silent any longer.

A Failure of Leadership

Although Senator John Kerry does not inspire a full measure of confidence, I cannot abide the deception that permeates the Bush administration. President George W. Bush has failed us in Iraq and must be held accountable.

I will credit Mr. Bush with taking strong, decisive steps, initially, in responding to the terrible attacks of September 11, 2001. At Ground Zero, he put his arm around a firefighter and vowed the terrorists would soon hear from us. I can't remember a more stirring moment. His decision to invade Afghanistan to wipe out al-Qaeda training camps was justified. I will accept that he did not lie to us about the reasons to launch a preemptive war against Iraq. I will believe he relied in good faith on grossly erroneous intelligence reports warning of a WMD stockpile and imminent threat to our national security.

But what I cannot excuse is Mr. Bush's lack of honesty now, when we need honesty. What I cannot forgive is the unwillingness to recognize and admit mistakes, a character trait of this president that promises to pay bitter dividends in the future. What I cannot overlook is the depth to which he has plunged American prestige in the world. What I condemn is the brazen choice to put his own reelection above his duty to lead us out of this mess. All of us, no matter what our political leanings, want the president to succeed in Iraq. But I no longer have confidence that George W. Bush is the right person to lead us to a place and time when we can truly say, "Mission accomplished."

Members of the president's own party are beginning to speak out. In recent weeks, three prominent Republican senators have criticized President Bush's handling of the war. Sen. Chuck Hagel of Nebraska said on "Face the Nation" last month, "The fact is, we're in deep trouble in Iraq . . . and I think we're going to have to look at some recalibration of policy." Sen. Richard Lugar of Indiana, chair of the Foreign Relations Committee, spoke of "incompetence in the [president's] administration." Sen. John McCain, commenting on the president's lack of candor with the American people, said Mr. Bush was "perhaps not as straight as maybe we'd like to see."

The president's mantra, now that WMD have not been found, is that Saddam Hussein was a brutal dictator and the world is a better place because of his removal. True, but at what price? More than 1,050 Americans dead? More than 7,000 Americans wounded? The world abounds with brutal regimes, some of which are much closer than Saddam Hussein was to possessing nuclear capabilities. Iran and North Korea spring to mind, yet they have been all but forgotten as we contend with Iraq. I shudder to think of the danger we face should one of these other countries develop into a hot spot while we are still embroiled in Iraq.

Just once I'd like us to elect a president who has read a history book, and I don't mean the Action Comic Book version. Far too often, our presidents have ignored the lessons of history, dooming thousands of young men, mostly, but now more and more women, to pay the price for their ignorance.

It's a failure of leadership that knows no partisan boundaries. The most obvious example is the Viet Nam debacle, in which Eisenhower, Kennedy, Johnson, and Nixon all had a hand. The *lesson* these leaders ignored? The Viet Namese had been natural enemies of the Chinese for a thousand years. Had we offered them economic aid when the French left, a united Viet Nam would probably have become if not a US ally, then at least a buffer against Chinese hegemony. More important, hundreds of thousands of

American lives—servicemen and their families—would not have been so terribly altered for all time in such an utter waste.

During the Viet Nam war, first President Johnson and then President Nixon spoke of "the light at the end of the tunnel," a promise of relief that never materialized. "VietNamitization" of the war— training the South Viet Namese to carry out their own defense—was supposed to be our way out with honor. It was a pipe dream. In a similar vein, President Bush says we are making progress in Iraq. We will train the Iraqis, he says, to take over responsibility for their own security. Perhaps, but it smacks of the false progress reports fed to us thirty years ago. I just don't see Iraqis putting aside centuries-old hatred and distrust of rival tribal and religious factions in order to work together in a harmonious, Western-style democracy.

The president and his advisors failed miserably at predicting the reaction of Iraqis and, for that matter, the whole Islamic world to an American invasion. We have been the *infidel* for centuries. Sunni and Shi'a Muslims have been blood enemies since the death of the prophet Mohammed 1400 years ago; perhaps the only thing they agree on is that they hate Americans more than they hate each other.

The president's claim that it is better to fight terrorism *over there*, rather than within our own borders, is a specious argument, designed to deflect attention from the realities we face. It is true that we have not suffered another attack within our borders since September 11, 2001, but that is purely a matter of luck. Our intelligence resources have not grown appreciably stronger or more cooperative with each other. Our borders are almost as porous as before. Our pseudo-security precautions at airports are a joke; grey-haired grandmothers and fresh-faced children are randomly selected for full body searches in a ridiculous observance of political correctness. Yet, little of the checked luggage that goes into passenger planes and less than 10% of shipping containers entering this country are inspected. In short, we are still a nation at risk. The report of the non-partisan 9/11 Commission confirms it.

President George W. Bush squandered an opportunity to go down in history as one of our greatest presidents. If only he had put aside what now seems like a predetermined notion to take out

Saddam Hussein. If only he had concentrated his efforts on hunting down Osama bin Laden and al-Qaeda. Here is the speech he should have delivered soon after September 11, 2001.

My fellow Americans. We have suffered the most grievous attack in our nation's history. Over the coming months and years, it will be necessary for me to make decisions that go against our most cherished ideals as Americans. I may have to ask you to give up some civil liberties, temporarily, so we may better protect ourselves against those who would destroy us. I may have to ask you to forego tax reforms that I had hoped would allow you to keep more of the money you work so hard to earn. I may have to ask you to endure even more hardships so that future generations of Americans can live in peace and security. With that in mind, I want to take politics off the table. In this most difficult time, I don't want you ever to worry about political considerations seeping into discussions about our future. I shall not be a candidate for reelection in 2004. The problems we face are too important for me to spend even a moment on politics. You elected me to lead you. That's what I intend to do over the next four years. Together, we shall meet this challenge. Together, we shall prevail.

Sadly, President George W. Bush has chosen a different course. We must be firm in our rejection of that course and of him.

Memorial Day Address—May 29, 2006

Memorial Day is a time when, traditionally, our nation's leaders put aside political differences to honor those who've died in service to their country. It is a day when we focus not on policies or decisions that led us into war, but rather on the men and women most directly affected by the consequences of those policies and decisions.

At the time of my first Memorial Day address as mayor three years ago, the Iraq War had claimed the lives of 160 men and one woman serving in the United States military. To honor those young heroes, I read all 161 names. Most were Americans, of course, but some were immigrants serving in the armed forces to gain citizenship and a better life. On this Memorial Day, the list of casualties—killed and wounded—has increased twenty-fold and is far too long for me to read at this ceremony. At last count, we have lost almost 2,500 dead and tens of thousands wounded in both Iraq and Afghanistan—half with wounds so grave they could not return to duty.

Twenty-five thousand Iraqi civilians have died, most as victims of their own countrymen—sectarian fanatics who would rather bring on a civil war bloodbath than see a rival religious faction in charge.

On the bronze tablets behind me, we've placed the names of Ramsey residents who served their country in time of war. Some are marked with a star, meaning they died in combat. The large monument in the center was erected to commemorate what was then called "the Great World War," before there was need for Roman numerals I and II. The inscription on the far side reads as follows:

We, the people of Ramsey, NJ, as a lasting expression of
our gratitude and affection have dedicated this memorial
as a testimonial to the young men of this community
who, in a spirit of unselfish patriotism, answered their
country's call in the Great World War.

The memorial lists the names of 48 Ramsey men who served during WWI. Five have gold stars: George Hemion, Toby Jannicelli, Alphonse Paglia, Herman Charles Stein, and Nicholas J. Stocker.

During the Second World War, 445 Ramsey residents served. To put that number in perspective, it would have been about 10% of our population at the time. Seven men did not return home: Arthur W. Edwards, A. L. Hanson, Arthur J. Margotte, Jr., George M. Maresca, Victor Matthews, F.W. Schierloh, Jr., for whom our VFW Post is named, and Henry S. Towne.

The third monument behind me has the 229 names of those who served during the Korean and Viet Nam wars. Eight were killed: Adamo DeAngelis, Donald Van Dine, Eric Magnuson, William Metzger, Richard Ovaitt, Paul Serven, and William Jones, whom I remember as Billy—an 18-year kid who taught me, a 10-year old, how to beat the pinball machine in my father's luncheonette on Main Street. Billy was a medic and died on a muddy battleground in Korea while helping a wounded comrade.

And, finally, Charles Hosking, a man who deserves special

mention. Master Sergeant Hosking, Ramsey's own Congressional Medal of Honor recipient, fell on a Viet Cong grenade to protect other soldiers at a command post and was awarded, posthumously, our country's highest decoration for bravery. Hosking had also fought in World War II and Korea, and thanks to the Ramsey PBA, he is honored with a special monument in this park.

The sad irony is that it often takes a war—and war dead—to make us appreciate the men and women who go in harm's way to keep our nation safe and free. In times of peace, the military has too often been ridiculed and neglected, left to languish in the backwater of our national consciousness. Enlisted personnel have been paid so poorly that some needed food stamps to feed their families. Equipment deteriorated or became outdated. Bases were closed. Aging, infirm veterans were packed off to nursing homes that left much to be desired in the quality of their care.

English poet Francis Quarles expressed the sentiment this way, four centuries ago:

> God and the soldier we adore,
> In times of danger, not before;
> The danger passed and all things righted,
> God is forgotten and the soldier slighted.

Faced with war, Americans have always risen to the occasion. World War I unveiled the remarkable military might of the United States and saw our country become a recognized world power. Teddy Roosevelt had started that process by sending the Great White Fleet around the world to display American naval strength, but it was American troops and tanks sent "Over There" to save Europe (for the first time) that elevated the U.S. to a first-rate power.

We disbanded our army and navy at the end of the First World War and returned to a policy of isolationism. Just before the Second World War began, our army ranked 17th or 18th in the world. December 7, 1941, changed everything.

Automobile production lines became tank and airplane production lines, "manned" by a workforce of Rosie Riveters. Freckle-faced farm boys, each a potential Alvin York, threw down pitchforks and took up rifles. City boys, mostly sons of immigrant parents, learned to march, drill and shoot. Together they formed the greatest land, air and sea Armada the world has ever known.

Winston Churchill knew without doubt that the American giant had been awakened, that the war's inevitable outcome had been decided the moment the Japanese attacked Pearl Harbor.

Amazingly, the transformation from peace and military weakness to war and military superiority was accomplished over a span of less than 18 months. Our ocean barriers gained us time to accomplish the feat—something we can no longer count on—but our national will was the deciding factor. It is a will aptly described in a passage from Shakespeare's *King Henry V*:

> In peace there's nothing so becomes a man
> As modest stillness and humility;
> But when the blast of war blows in our ears,
> Then imitate the action of the tiger;
> Stiffen the sinews, summon up the blood,
> Disguise fair nature with hard-favored rage;
> Then lend the eye a terrible aspect.

We still have the national will to be a force for good in this world, despite our tendency at times to misplace it. I end my Memorial Day speech today in the same way I ended three years ago:

"The Iraq War is testament to the skill and bravery of American men and women, if not to the intelligence gathering capabilities of certain government agencies or the judgment of certain politicians. Let us resolve on this Memorial Day to always be prepared to go to war when our national interests require it, but to always strive for peaceful solutions to world crises that confront us. As John Milton put it, 'Peace hath her victories, no less renowned than War'."

Chapter 19

This Op-Ed article appeared in The Record on Sunday, April 11, 2004, on page 1 of the Opinion Section, above the fold. In the piece, I explain why I was disassociating myself from the Bergen County Democratic Organization. I remained a Democrat for the time being, but chose to describe myself as an "Independent" Democrat.

This stand ultimately cost me reelection in November 2006. Republicans nominated the council president as their candidate— an attractive young family man, who had been a frequent supporter of my reform agenda. Not wanting to be part of the Bergen County Democratic Organization ticket, I ran for a second term as an Independent. The Democratic machine put up a straw- man candidate to siphon off votes from me by making it a three- way race.

I lost to the Republican by 189 votes, out of more than 5,000 cast. The Democratic candidate finished a distant third, but managed to poll about 800 votes. That was enough to insure my defeat. The county chairman I had spoken out against in this article got his revenge.

P.S. I'd do the same thing all over again.

One Mayor's Declaration of Independence

As a political novice in November 2002, I won a landslide victory and became Ramsey's first Democratic mayor in sixteen years. Today, with sadness, I renounce any affiliation with the Bergen County Democratic Party; henceforth, I shall consider myself an

Independent Democrat and shall no longer participate in any party functions in this county. I take this action not for political gain, but for the sole purpose of demonstrating my opposition to the leadership of the Democratic Party Organization in Bergen County and the direction in which that leadership is taking us.

Anyone who has followed my public life might reasonably conclude that I have a quixotic tendency. I admit the flaw. Four years ago as deputy first assistant prosecutor for administration, I wrote a letter to county officials suggesting that my boss, the Bergen County Prosecutor, was about to waste millions in public funds to purchase a building we didn't need to house an ever-increasing staff we didn't need. I was fired that same day, ending a nineteen year career as a prosecutor just ten months shy of qualifying for retirement health benefits. The building was purchased without further scrutiny, and the prosecutor's staff continued to grow.

Last year, I ran an expensive and mostly self-financed campaign for state senate against the entrenched Gerald Cardinale, without having much impact on his traditional winning margins. That windmill-tilting episode left me with a big second mortgage that, at age 64, I will be paying the rest of my life.

This public "declaration of independence" will likely be just as futile. The pay-to-play mentality that has gripped the Democratic Party under Chairman Joseph Ferriero, arguably the most powerful man in Bergen County, will continue to flourish. He is, after all, a winner. He delivered Democrats from the political wilderness and put them in control of county government. Not just the freeholder board, but the office of county executive as well. State senators owe their existence to him. One word from the Chairman, and senatorial courtesy will block any state appointment not to his liking. As a result, Ferriero controls all patronage in the largest county in New Jersey.

In Ramsey, a town Mr. Ferriero does not control, we had an opening for borough attorney earlier this year. The Chairman's firm, Scarinci & Hollenbeck, wanted the position. My appointment of someone else did not endear me to the Chairman, but a few weeks later I committed a much more grievous offense. I wrote a letter of support for Regina O'Neill, the independent-minded Democrat who challenged Ferriero's hand-picked candidates for freeholder at last month's party convention.

On convention night, the party faithful lined up behind the Chairman by a wide margin. I was shunned by most of those present, people who had hailed me just a year earlier as the new hope for Democrats in northwest Bergen County. A few brave souls managed a furtive smile, hoping, I'm sure, to avoid notice by the Chairman's cell phone-toting operatives in the hall. I was content to let the matter end there, without further public comment. Then I received a letter from the "Bergen County Democratic Senators." It was the last straw.

The letter, signed by Senators Byron Baer, Joseph Coniglio and Paul Sarlo, urged county Democrats to get behind our Chairman. It praised Ferriero's "unprecedented success in electing Democrats at all levels of government." It castigated those "who have questioned the incredible gains Bergen Democrats have made in recent years." It condemned those who have "questioned our core values as Democrats and have unsuccessfully sought to create a rift in what should be a unified Democratic Party built on a record of success."

I expected more from senators, especially one of Byron Baer's stature. Senator Baer was and is one of my political heroes. He was a civil rights pioneer, marching shoulder to shoulder down South with other giants of the movement when it was dangerous to do so, physically and politically. He risked life and limb trying to help migrant farm workers in South Jersey. He has been the driving force in the New Jersey legislature, first as assemblyman and then as senator, for a multitude of reform measures. He is a true and courageous champion of the people. I am heartsick that he, too, feels constrained to jump through Ferriero's hoops.

In my letter for O'Neill, I wrote: "The greatest tragedy that could befall the Democratic Party in this county . . . would be to abandon the moral high ground to Republicans. Sadly, I think we are in danger of doing just that." I said, perhaps a bit too melodramatically, that the convention process pitting O'Neill against the Chairman's candidates was a "struggle for the soul of our party" in Bergen County.

It sometimes seems as though we *have* sold our soul to the highest contributor. I'm tired of reading about no-bid contracts for professional services going to "pay-to-players" who have filled coffers at party headquarters. Solemn pronouncements about appointments being made without regard to campaign contributions—law firms or engineering companies or politically connected individuals getting the jobs always happen to be the "best qualified"—would be comical if they weren't so telling about the health of our body politic. When Republicans were in power, I'm not sure it was any different.

Theodore Sorensen, President Kennedy's speech writer, put it well in his book, *Why I Am a Democrat*:

> Even more important than winning another election, the Democratic Party must *deserve* to win and thereby gain not merely a brief interlude between periods of Republican control, not merely a backlash victory as a result of Republican overreaching and self-destruction, but a return to the long-term sustainable public esteem and confidence that the party long enjoyed in the past.

But what have we seen in recent years? A Sheriff selling honorary badges for campaign contributions is convicted of criminal wrongdoing and forced from office. With a last-minute infusion of big money from out-of-county sources, the McNerney campaign launches a negative mail attack against Senator Hank McNamara in the county executive race. Gary Funari is maneuvered out of his state senate seat (with a judgeship as bait) so the more attractive Paul Sarlo can take over. Matt Ahearn, a principled, courageous young legislator is driven from the party for not toeing the line.

I'm not sure Democrats in Bergen County still deserve to win.

Chapter 20

I was invited by Professor Murray Sabrin, Director of the Center for Business and Public Policy, Ramapo College of New Jersey, to take part in a symposium on campaign finance reform. The other panelists were announced candidates for governor of New Jersey, and I felt honored to be part of the discussion. I gave these opening remarks on May 9, 2005.

Campaign Finance Reform:
Can the Culture of Corruption be Abolished?

The question before this symposium is, "Campaign Finance Reform: Can the 'Culture of Corruption' Be Abolished?" Unfortunately, I think the honest answer to that question is, "Probably not." For two reasons.

First, the public in general doesn't give a damn. They are too involved in the "runaway bride" saga, the Michael Jackson trial, American Idol hanky-panky, and other manifestations of the popular culture. They don't read newspapers or give serious attention to anything that doesn't affect their lives, immediately and directly.

Fewer than half of registered voters bother to vote, unless it is a presidential election year, when slightly more turn out. Those who do vote are ill-informed about the issues, gaining what little information they have from superficial television news coverage or, worse, from the deluge of slick television ads or direct mail by well-financed candidates. Usually, this onslaught of mind-numbing inanities comes in the final weeks before Election Day; candidates know the public's short attention span.

Ads are crafted by experts, the content test-marketed before focus groups. The object is to create a positive image for the candidate, or to besmirch the opponent, fairly or unfairly—it doesn't matter. Nothing of substance will be said in those ads, despite the gravity of the problems we face—problems with no pat answers or easy solutions. Instead, the candidate will spew forth platitudes designed to perpetuate the notion of a "free lunch." We can have everything we want, without sacrifice or higher taxes, if only we will give the candidate a chance to root out waste, fraud, and abuses in Trenton.

If you think I'm wrong about public apathy, I suggest you look at Bergen County, well on its way to becoming an affluent suburban version of Tammany Hall. The Democratic Party here has a strangle-hold on county government, controlling the county executive position, six of seven freeholder seats, the sheriff's office, and the county prosecutor's office. The county administrator is a former McGreevey operative from the city of Woodbridge. How did Democrats go from the political wilderness to this pinnacle of power? Money, and the genius of the Democratic Party chairman in dispensing patronage and no-bid contracts in a way that will keep the campaign cash spigot flowing freely. He has raised "pay-to-play" to an art form.

The Bergen *Record* has devoted gallons of ink and tons of newsprint to exposing this state of affairs, but to what end. The problem persists. Relatively few citizens bother to read the in-depth coverage. In the last election, three Democratic freeholder candidates were elected in a walk, strengthening party control of that board.

In a way, politics has become farce. In the county executive race three years ago, the Democratic candidate ran on a platform of ending pay-to-play and bringing about campaign finance reform. Then, weeks before that election, the county chair wheeled in millions from outside Bergen and launched a blitzkrieg that buried the Republican candidate, a respected state senator. What became of the promised campaign finance reform? You guessed it—nothing. When hounded by the press about his unkept promise in that regard, the county executive appointed a panel to study the problem. Nothing has been heard from them since.

In the sheriff's race last year, the Republican incumbent was chastised for exceeding his overtime budget, despite the fact that he had warned freeholders they were allocating too little for that line item. After the Democratic candidate was victorious, the freeholders increased the Sheriff Department's overtime budget significantly. Before the election, the freeholder board, amid much fanfare, hired a Democratic campaign contributor to investigate the Republican Sheriff's financial arrangements for housing federal detainees, claiming they were costing county taxpayers money. After the election, we learned, quietly, that the arrangement for housing those federal detainees was, indeed, quite beneficial for the county. The former sheriff had been right all along.

Do you honestly think that politicians, whose source of power is not the quality of their ideas for governing, but rather the money they can raise—do you honestly think those politicians will ever do anything voluntarily to undermine their source of power?

That brings me to my second reason for pessimism about chances for reform. Rarely, if ever, will politicians go against their self interests. The enactment of true reform must come from Trenton, but both parties know they are safe under the current system. Incumbents attract the campaign contributions of special interest groups and are rarely defeated for reelection. Why would they ever give challengers a leg up by evening the playing field? If a challenger succeeds nowadays, it is because he or she did the incumbent one better. In the 4th legislative district in 2003, the Democratic challenger spent $4 million to unseat a shaky Republican incumbent, who *only* spent $1 million. Control of the state senate was at stake, so money poured in from everywhere to elect the man. Do you think that newly elected senator will be a champion of campaign finance reform?

I was invited to speak at this symposium as the token Democrat, to bring balance to the picture. Yet, here I am bashing mostly Democrats. But Democrats are not solely to blame. Republicans did little to change the system when they were in power. "The fault, dear Brutus, is not in our stars, but in ourselves." I can name the guilty party for you, but in doing so I must refer to one of my favorite philosophers, someone who was celebrated in the 1940s and -50s for his political wisdom. Wearing a paper admiral's hat and raising a wooden sword on high, Pogo, the intrepid opossum, stood in the prow of his leaky rowboat and declared to the world, "We have met the enemy, and he is us." Until the public consciousness is awakened, to the extent that we are motivated to demand change and won't take "no" for an answer, the current morally corrupt system will continue. Our state, and our children's heritage, will be the poorer for it.

Chapter 21

Governor Jim McGreevey left office in disgrace, not for being a "gay American," as he proclaimed himself to be, but for appointing his paramour to a position of trust for which he was not qualified. Despite that sordid episode, I praised the governor in this "In the Arena" column for taking a good government stand as one of his final acts in office. He signed an executive order banning "pay-to-play," an insidious practice that corrupts politics at every level. In November 2003, the Borough of Ramsey became the first municipality in Bergen County to adopt its own local ordinance against pay-to-play. Using a model ordinance from New Jersey Common Cause as a guide, I wrote that law and proposed it to the council, which passed it unanimously.

Taking Aim at Legalized Corruption

In a striking move last week, Governor James E. McGreevey issued an executive order banning the practice of "pay-to-play" in state government. It was something he had promised during his successful election campaign in 2001, but he never got around to it until now, seven weeks before he is to leave office in disgrace. Had the governor taken this bold initiative a few months into his administration, when there was everything to lose and nothing to gain, it would have been a courageous act. Still, one cannot discount this significant step toward reducing legalized corruption in New Jersey.

That's exactly what "pay-to-play" is—legalized corruption. Here's how it works.

State, county and local governments must follow bidding laws in awarding most public contracts. That means they must give the contract to the company offering to do the work for the lowest price. There are ways around that, of course. For example, bid specifications can be rigged so that only one company (the favored one) has the ability to fulfill them. But that aside, the requirement to choose the lowest responsible bidder usually does save taxpayers money.

There is one important exception to the low bid rule. Providers of certain services—like lawyers, engineers, architects, and other skilled professions—do not have to follow the bidding process. They can be awarded contracts at the discretion of politicians with decision-making power for that particular project, be they local council members, county freeholders, state legislators or the governor.

As a consequence of this exception, money in the form of campaign contributions flows freely. The only brake on it is a limit of $2,200 that any one person or company can give to any one candidate—so-called "hard money." A way around it, and the path followed by every seasoned practitioner of the pay-to-play game, is the "soft money" approach.

No-bid professionals and others hoping for a sweetheart contract can give up to $37,000 a year to a county political committee. That's real money, and the folks who play in that league are often rewarded with public contracts worth hundreds of thousands, if not millions.

If these professionals had given money directly to a candidate to influence his or her official action, that would have been bribery, a crime. But the contribution to a political campaign, ostensibly with no strings attached (wink, wink), is perfectly legal. As one county political boss put it in a quote to *The Record* last week, people give to his organization "because they believe in what our party is doing." Believe that, and I've got a nice bridge over in Brooklyn I'd like to sell you.

The governor's edict will have an effect on pay-to-play at the state level, but it may not have legs at county or local levels. Time will tell. It depends on whether or not county and local politicians feel there is strong public sentiment for a house-cleaning. In other words, it depends on you.

County Executive Dennis McNerney, emboldened by the

governor's move, has announced that he is considering a similar action in Bergen County. First, he wants to research the issue to make sure he does it right. There is nothing wrong with that. Freeholder chairperson Valerie Huttle says she will encourage McNerney to follow through. Folks, this may be the start of something big.

By the way, the Borough of Ramsey was in the good government forefront on this issue. We enacted our own local ordinance outlawing pay-to-play almost one year ago. Every council member voted in favor of our proposal, which was based on the New Jersey Common Cause model ordinance. We were the first municipality in Bergen County to pass a law in this regard and the tenth or eleventh in the state.

The Ramsey ordinance sets a limit of $400. No professional who hopes to get a no-bid contract in the Borough of Ramsey can contribute more than that amount to any municipal candidate or candidate committee. Once a professional is employed by the borough or is negotiating for employment, he or she may not contribute anything at all to municipal candidates—not a dime.

I think Governor McGreevey acted honorably when he signed this executive order banning pay-to-play at the state level. It was a noble thing to do. Sure, he hopes to repair his tarnished image, but so what. Perhaps this was the only way to get something done. Politicians craving reelection are not noted for their political courage. McGreevey, with no hope of ever being elected again to any post, was the right man in the right place at the right time. Good for him.

Chapter 22

"There he goes again," my detractors might very well have said after reading this piece, "sticking his nose where it doesn't belong." This time I paid for the space to do it. I took out a two-page ad in the local paper. The school board was proposing a $26 million bond issue to build new facilities. I agreed with most of their proposal, except for their plan to tear down an old school— the Dater School—and replace it with a new building. I felt we could have saved $8 to $10 million by making improvements to the older building, which still had a lot of use left, according to experts I talked to. In the end, I advocated support for the referendum, but not before taking the school board to task for their scare tactics.

A Reluctant "Yes" Vote on the School Bond Referendum

I will vote yes on the school bond referendum September 30th, but will do so with a touch of anger over the tactics used by some bond proponents, great sadness over the loss of a venerable and still usable building, and a vow to continue scrutinizing the school board's stewardship of our money.

Let me preface my remarks by stating my belief that Ramsey school board members and administrators are honorable people trying to do the right thing. Where I am critical of their actions, my criticism is directed at their judgment, not their integrity. They have done well in establishing the quality of educational opportunities in Ramsey, but apparently fail to realize or acknowledge that we are on the cusp of a new economic reality in this municipality, this state and this country. For those who ignore the overwhelming evidence of drastic changes ahead, the consequences will be severe.

Just 17 days ago, President Bush announced that it will take another $87 billion to finish the job in Iraq, not counting the $79 billion we have already spent. This comes on top of record federal deficits, a seemingly untouchable tax cut program that will reduce federal revenue by hundreds of billions more in the next decade, and a War on Terrorism that may present the most frightening and costly specter of all. The Department of Homeland Security has said that another terrorist attack in the United States is likely. God forbid it should ever come, but imagine the new havoc it will wreak on our economy, the already high unemployment rate, the stock market, and people's life savings.

According to *The New York Times*, the cumulative federal deficit will, over the next eight years, reach $2.3 trillion. Yes, trillion. We don't have the money, of course, so it will have to be borrowed, causing interest rates to soar and further complicating any hope for a quick economic recovery. Who will pay the bill? Our children and our children's children.

Twenty years ago, the federal government promised to fund mandated special education programs at 40% of their cost. It has never come close to that promised level of funding. Only recently has its support risen to 19% nationwide, but for us folks in so-called affluent districts, we see just 6% of our special education costs reimbursed by the federal government. Given the bleak financial outlook, the Feds will never reach their promised level of support. Never. And what's more, they will most likely reduce aid in every other category, leaving the states in a greater financial bind than they are in now.

New Jersey is in the midst of its most severe financial crisis since the Great Depression. In his first two years in office, Governor McGreevey has had to deal with $14 billion in budget deficits. The budget this year was balanced with the help of, among other things, a one-time advance of $1.6 billion in tobacco litigation settlement money. Next year, that Band-Aid will not be available, and we face another $4 or 5 billion deficit. That means less property tax relief, less aid to municipalities, less aid to schools.

With regard to Ramsey's municipal budget, which accounts for

23% of your property tax dollar, we will be in good shape next year no matter what Trenton throws at us. That's because a majority of the borough council (two Republicans and two Democrats) and I saw what was coming and planned for it. We've cut operating expenses and have retained a $5+ million surplus to cushion the blow. With regard to the county portion of your tax dollar (10%), I don't expect much, if any, increase there.

What worries me is the ever growing school portion of your taxes, which accounts this year for 67% of every property tax dollar and which, given current trends, will grow to 70% or more in the next few years. Salaries and benefits make up almost 80% of the school budget, and the 3-year contract the school board just gave teachers (average 4.45% raise each year, with no reduction in health insurance benefits or contribution toward their cost) will guarantee substantial tax increases for the foreseeable future. Health insurance expense is going up 20% a year, with no relief in sight. Even if next year's school tax increase were to stay the same as this year's (highly unlikely), that and the debt service to pay for the bond proposal will result at least a $500 property tax increase for the average home in Ramsey ($415,000 in assessed value).

I do not think school officials considered the harsh economic future that confronts us when they conceived their school facilities plan. I think they simply went for the "Cadillac" option, instead of giving fair and unbiased consideration to the "Chevrolet" option. The problem is, it may be too late to do anything about it.

I am angry over the Dater School issue because we have been backed into a corner. When I hear a board member characterize Dater School as a "firetrap," my blood boils. The school is well sprinklered and meets all applicable fire codes, according to experts. Does anyone honestly believe the Board of Education would have allowed children to attend school for the last few decades in a firetrap? Would it continue the use of Dater for another two years during construction of a new school if Dater were a firetrap? What other purpose could that board member have had but to scare parents into submission? Predictions of plaster falling on children's heads, signs of rodent infestation, claims of a flooded gymnasium, and cries of "substandard" classrooms all contributed to an atmosphere in which it was difficult to make a rational decision. Lately, we've been warned that our property values will plummet if we say no to the bond referendum.

The last time the gym had a water problem was 18 years ago. Hurricane Floyd came and went without notice at the Dater School gym. One teacher had kids glue Cheerios to poster paper and stored the project in her classroom; it drew field mice. "Substandard" is a worrisome word, but it simply means smaller than the recommended size for new classrooms. The remedy is smaller class sizes, not a bad thing. Plaster can be repaired and maintained.

And what about those warnings of split sessions and sending children to school in trailers if we were to pursue a rehabilitation alternative? Were those the only solutions to the problem of housing children during the rehab? I don't think so. Hubbard School, Smith School, and the high school are all scheduled to be expanded as part of this bond proposal. Tisdale School was just recently expanded. Couldn't we have done the other projects first, then moved children around to other schools while the Dater rehab proceeded? Even if we couldn't have accommodated all the children in that fashion, what about leasing space in another building to temporarily house the overflow? Why can't we consider creative solutions to our problems for a change, rather than threatening the most expensive, least attractive alternatives?

The folks who served on the Board of Education's school facilities committee were trying to do the right thing for our kids. We all want to do the right thing for our kids, but must we always take the most expensive approach? Were any of those folks on the committee seniors living on a fixed income? Were any of them struggling to make ends meet with both parents working, perhaps more than one job? I don't think so.

During my campaign for mayor, I promised that I would speak out on issues of importance, including school issues that impact on property taxes. Some school board members see me as an interloper and have jealously guarded their turf. When I asked for a second opinion last November [regarding the cost to rehabilitate, as opposed to new construction], I was ignored. When I followed up with a written request to the school board president in February 2003, it was ignored. When I took out a full-page ad in a local newspaper setting forth my concerns in March 2003, I was attacked.

Question the Board of Education's pronouncements on what is in the best interests of our children and risk being branded an enemy of education. This BOE can do no wrong in the minds of its militant followers, and I am certain that this published statement of my position will unleash a torrent of letters to the editor against me and some of the same type of hate mail I have received in the past. One woman called with this anonymous message: "Mayor Muti, if you care so much about the poor people, why don't you move to Paterson with all the dot-heads and niggers." I still have the tape and will keep it as a humbling reminder that I will never be able to reach everyone. But that woman's hateful message does not sadden me half as much as the intolerance displayed by far too many others—people who should know better—over my attempt to get fair consideration of less expensive alternatives. It's sad that we've reached this point. I suppose I could have just kept silent, as past mayors have done. But I would have abdicated my responsibility, I think, had I taken that route. I think it is healthy to ask questions— indeed, to demand responsive answers to those questions and not be put off by a wave of the hand or a changing of the subject or the disapproval of a hand-picked audience. We need to question government officials at every level, including school boards.

Why, after this lengthy rejection of the school board's procedures, judgment and tactics, do I still express my intention to vote "yes" on the school bond referendum? Because I believe the school superintendent when he says it may be too late to do anything else. Given the state's fiscal house of cards, school facilities funding may disappear in the not too distant future. Even if we were able to come up with a viable alternative that would save five or six million dollars—not likely given the present makeup of the school board— we might lose five or six million in state aid if we went back to the planning stage now.

It's too late to do anything about Dater, I'm afraid. Too late, perhaps, to find a vacant piece of land, either at one of the other school sites or at another suitable location, thereby saving demolition costs and gaining revenue from the sale of the School Street property to help offset the cost of new construction. Too late to find out what Saddle River is doing before we commit ourselves. Too late to see what other creative approaches people might suggest. And that is

a shame. But perhaps we can salvage some good out of this mess.
Perhaps we can move forward in a spirit of tolerance instead of
close-mindedness, of cooperation instead of recrimination. We
must learn to do that if we hope to preserve the character of this
wonderful community.

Chapter 23

Another "In the Arena" article.

A Nation of 'History-phobes'

Two polls conducted for this Presidents' Day show how little we Americans know about the men who led our country and, by implication, the history of our great nation.

According to an Associated Press news item in the February 21st edition of *The Record*, separate polls were commissioned by Washington College in Maryland and by the CNN-USA Today-Gallup group. Both asked respondents to choose the "greatest" presidents.

In the college's poll, George Washington was ranked seventh. Among those placed ahead of "the father of our country" were Bill Clinton, George H.W. Bush (of "read my lips" fame), John F. Kennedy, and Ronald Reagan. Lincoln topped the list, so at least they got one right. Franklin D. Roosevelt, who led us through the Great Depression and the most devastating war in the history of the world, barely secured third place, beating Kennedy and Clinton by a nose.

Fewer than half the people knew George Washington led our army during the Revolutionary War, or knew his wife's name was Martha, or knew he lived at Mount Vernon.

Results in the CNN-USA Today-Gallup poll were worse, if that's possible. Lincoln finished a dismal third, behind Ronald Reagan (the choice of one out of every five respondents as our greatest president) and behind—you're going to love this—Bill Clinton, who finished second. FDR and Kennedy tied for fourth, and Washington tied for sixth.

Are you as outraged by this as I am? Probably not. I can imagine many of you muttering, "Get over it, Mayor Muti."

Okay, I admit I'm a history nut. It was a favorite subject throughout my public school days in Ramsey. It seemed like American history and "civics" were emphasized more in those days. For our eighth grade graduation from Ramsey Elementary School (that venerable building we now call Dater School, soon to meet the wrecking ball), the Board of Education presented each student with a bound, hardcover book entitled, "Our Great State Papers." It included the U.S. Constitution, the Declaration of Independence, and the New Jersey Constitution. I still have my copy.

I had read every history book in the small school library before leaving for high school. Elementary school plays were about great historical figures. One of my proudest moments was playing the role of Abraham Lincoln, complete with fake whiskers and stovepipe hat. I had to memorize the Gettysburg Address. Actually, I was the understudy, who rose to 'greatness' when the first choice for that starring role got a tummy ache.

At Ramsey High School, Seelig Lewitz, my favorite teacher, made social studies class fun. Here's a brief example I still remember. Commenting on the process that gave Franklin Pierce the Democratic nomination for president in 1852—it took 48 ballots before Pierce was selected as the 'dark horse' candidate—Mr. Lewitz described it this way: "Franklin Pierce showed up at the Democratic convention looking for a free ham sandwich and ended up becoming the fourteenth president of the United States." I know it's obscure, but history nuts remember stuff like that.

Today, I teach American government and politics part time at Fairleigh Dickinson University. As you might imagine, history and the presidents make up much of the course. The pay isn't great, but the job comes with benefits like these anonymous comments from students at the end of last semester: "Mayor Muti is a great teacher"; "He explains things thoroughly—nobody's opinion is wrong—even if you participate and have a wrong answer, he will not make you feel stupid"; "If I have the opportunity to take Prof. Muti again, I will."

Lest these accolades go to my head, one student encouraged me to try harder. When asked to describe the least appealing aspect of the course, the student said, "the monotonous lectures."

Chapter 24

More Budgetary Woes: Trenton Officials Foresee Austere Financial Future

On January 21st I attended Mayors' Legislative Day in Trenton, an annual event sponsored by the NJ League of Municipalities. About a hundred mayors descended on our state capital to learn firsthand from legislators, department heads, and the governor what financial help we can expect in the next state budget. The answer? We will likely be funded at the same level as 2001, making 2004 the third year in a row with no increase in state aid. Department of Community Affairs Commissioner Susan Bass Levin urged local governments and school boards to put their own houses in order and cut expenses wherever possible. We can expect little help from the state, which faces another $4 to 5 billion deficit in next fiscal year's budget (July 2004 to June 2005) with no *quick fix* tobacco litigation money to help balance it. It wasn't news to me—I've been predicting just that financial picture for almost a year.

In his first two years in office, Governor McGreevey has had to deal with the largest cumulative deficits in New Jersey history—about $19 billion spread over four budgets. I admire the way he has grappled with that problem and don't understand why the public isn't more appreciative of his efforts. He has kept discretionary spending increases below the rate of inflation. Sure, there have been missteps, but it's hard to believe anyone could have done better under present circumstances. Let's give the man credit for hanging in there.

At the mayors' event, McGreevey talked about the need to consolidate, to regionalize government services and achieve efficiencies not possible with administrative redundancies and duplication of services. The governor is right, but it is a solution that is years away. New Jerseyans are too caught up with the idea of "home rule," something I support so long as we approach the issue rationally. Here in Ramsey, we are not even ready to talk about consolidating services within our own community, let alone the surrounding area. As property taxes continue to rise, we will be forced to talk about more creative solutions to the problems we face.

Another man who impressed me at the Mayors' Legislative Day was Senator Leonard Lance, the new Republican Minority Leader from Hunterdon County. It is readily apparent that Senator Lance is a man of integrity, and I am hopeful he will show the leadership necessary to put partisanship aside and make our state government work.

Among the things Senator Lance talked about were school funding and school budget issues. Senator Lance has tried for years to get a law passed that would move school budgets and Board of Education elections to November, when higher voter turnout would insure greater citizen participation in decisions that affect 67% of the property taxes we pay.

It makes sense, doesn't it? There is just one problem. School boards and the New Jersey Education Association (NJEA—the teachers' union) are dead set against moving school voting from its present April schedule, when, if we are lucky, 20% of the electorate participate. The vested interests don't want big voter turnouts because school budgets might then be defeated more often. School boards and teachers might have to make do with less.

Here in Ramsey, the Board of Education, with its telephone chain in full operation, can count on 2,000 votes at any school election, or general election, for that matter. That is enough to pass any measure and elect to public office anyone who is a "team player." It is also enough to defeat any local government candidate who dares to question the school board's decisions.

At the state level, NJEA is the most powerful union in New Jersey—even more powerful than the National Rifle Association. Its political action committee makes campaign contributions to about 90% of state legislators. Politicians don't usually bite the hand that feeds them. But the real power of the NJEA is the militancy of its large membership. These are folks who don't give an inch on what they consider to be their entitlements. And they vote as a block.

When NJEA speaks, politicians listen. This was readily apparent last June, when both houses of our legislature quickly and quietly passed a law to give teachers' unions more power in negotiating labor contracts. Under this law, it will be practically impossible for any school board to reduce health insurance benefits—the fastest growing line item in every school budget. It will probably cost most municipalities—Ramsey included—millions over the next 10 years.

We have to do a lot better with funding education costs. A constitutional convention is necessary, not only to look at the revenue side of public education (property taxes), but also the cost side. Governor McGreevey and Senator Lance are in agreement on that issue, so perhaps we may finally see action.

We also must reexamine the Abbott district dilemma. Thirty school districts (so-called "Abbott" districts, after the NJ Supreme Court decision that vastly altered our educational funding landscape) receive half the state aid to education. About 580 districts receive the other half. Every New Jersey youngster deserves a "thorough and efficient" education, a constitutional term the Supreme Court has defined as that which the most affluent school district provides to its children. In other words, if the richest district spends lavishly on extra-curricular activities and other education expenses because its taxpayers can afford it, then the rest of us must fund Abbott districts at the same level as those rich folks. Abbott districts should be funded at the state average, not at the level of the most affluent school districts. And we must take a close look at which districts fall under the Abbott umbrella. Hoboken, for example, represented by a powerful Democratic state senator, is classified as an Abbott district. Yet, with the influx of yuppies into its gentrified residential districts, its per capita income is above the state average. Why are Ramsey taxpayers subsidizing Hoboken schools?

State legislators have to remove reelection considerations from their thinking. They've got to start acting like statesmen, not politicians.

Chapter 25

A Look Back at Ramsey's Finances—96 years ago

In one week, Ramsey will celebrate its 96th birthday. On March 10, 1908, the state legislature enacted a law establishing Ramsey as a borough and carving our 5.6 square miles from the greater Hohokus Township. When we reach our Centennial in four years, I hope we will experience a full year of celebration. More than 20 volunteers on the Centennial Committee, under the leadership of former Mayor John Scerbo, have started the process to insure a successful commemoration in 2008 of Ramsey's official beginnings.

In thinking about our history, especially now during the budget season, I thought it might be fun to take a look at Ramsey's finances almost a century ago. Our chief financial officer found in the archives a copy of the borough's "Financial Report" for the year ended December 31, 1908. Four hundred copies were printed, enough to mail one to every taxpayer, but I'm not sure how many survive.

The total value of all real estate in Ramsey in 1908 was $521,285, as compared to a total value of about $2.7 billion today. Everything is relative, I guess. Then, as now, there was pressure to provide more municipal services using less money. Washed out roads were the chief problem. Except for parts of Franklin Turnpike that had been "macadamized," mostly dirt roads traversed our town. Main Street was often a quagmire in spring and summer in those early days, according to my father, right up to the time it was paved in the 1920's.

The Financial Report specified that $2,000 had been spent on road repairs, but, apparently, complaints were still coming in to borough hall. Town fathers, sensitive to the issue, made this statement: "The Mayor and Council realizing the importance of this work to the entire Borough regret that the limited funds in hand have not enabled them to make more extensive improvements." I may memorialize that comment for future use.

Aside from roads, some of the more interesting expenditures for 1908 were new handcuffs and badge for the town marshal ($6.50); purchase of a lock and road signs ($15.70); cleaning of the jail cells ($1.00); reimbursement to C.R. Rhoades for purchase of a mattress, pail and lantern ($3.20); and "typewriting" services provided by R.J. Minion ($6.60).

The names of property tax deadbeats, including prominent citizens of the time, were printed in the Financial Report, along with the amounts owed. James Shuart, a councilman, owed a dollar from 1907 and a dollar from 1908. Seth Wanamaker, who was still alive when I was a boy, owed the enormous sum of $48.25. Poor Abram Blauvelt couldn't escape the tax collector even in death. He was being dunned posthumously for 94 cents.

According to a July 22, 1908 edition of *The News*, a local weekly, the borough council fixed the tax rate at $1.38 per hundred of valuation. That would have made the total tax levy about $7,200, compared to more than $50 million today. The appropriated items in 1908 were $75 for the borough clerk's office; $125 for the assessor; $125 for the tax collector; $100 for attorneys' fees; $100 for the board of health; $465 for electricity; $1,500 for roads; $125 for the hospital; $50 for the marshal's office; $100 for printing; and $135 for "incidentals."

The $1.38 tax rate represented a 19% increase over the prior year, a rise that was almost entirely attributed to the higher cost of schools. Sound familiar? Of course, the consistent quality of Ramsey's schools over the years had a great deal to do with our valuation increasing from half a million to over $2.7 billion.

The 1908 article in *The News* ends with this interesting quote: "While the council was in session, it was interrupted several times by reports of rowdies making a disturbance in the village. The matter was thoroughly discussed and methods suggested and taken to prevent such occurrences in future."

I suspect that more marshal's badges and handcuffs made it into the 1909 budget.

Chapter 26

Another "In the Arena" column.

Report from Annapolis

Driving south on the New Jersey Turnpike, I tune to a Philadelphia radio station playing songs from the Sixties. How appropriate, I think, as I head toward Annapolis, my second favorite town, and the 40th reunion of the Class of 1964.

We get together every five years, my classmates and I—fewer in number each time, a little harder of hearing, a bit wider amidships. When we entered the Naval Academy in the summer of 1960, almost fourteen hundred of us, proud parents and grandparents looking on, took the oath and swore to defend our country against all enemies. Four years later, about nine hundred made it through the rigorous program. Each service academy likes to think of itself as the toughest, but all are comparable. There is no more exacting 4-year college experience in America—in terms of academic excellence, physical requirements, and military discipline—than that received at West Point, Annapolis or Colorado Springs.

Perhaps that is why we are drawn back to each reunion. I don't think I've missed one of them. This year, six hundred of my classmates attended, the largest gathering of any class in the 159-year history of the Academy. All are retired from military service now. Some, like me, left as soon as our obligated service was fulfilled to pursue civilian careers in business, medicine, law, and other professions. Others made the military their career, mostly in the Navy and Marine Corps, but a few in the Air Force and Army, too. Our last man in uniform, Admiral Connie Lautenbacher, retired in

2000, after 36 years on active duty, "the last man ashore." In all, we had twenty admirals, two generals, a Secretary of the Navy, an ambassador to China, and a Commandant of the Marine Corps. Five classmates had the distinction of having been involuntary "guests" of Ho Chi Minh at the Hanoi Hilton.

No matter what our career choice, no matter what distinctions classmates may have earned, we are a band of brothers bonded by our common experience at the Academy, our universal support of the military, and our unflagging love of country.

That is not to say we don't disagree on politics. While we were in the service, political discussions were banned in the wardroom of every ship, as were discussions of women and religion. Those were the three taboo subjects. It was a precaution strictly enforced to insure harmony in close quarters. But in this election season, politics was on the minds of most of us at the reunion. Although we talked the subject to death, no minds were changed.

It was a great time for reminiscing, too. Everyone had sea stories to tell of our days at "Canoe U.," or the "boat school," two affectionate names for our *alma mater*. No one minded a little exaggeration now and then, a little "filling in" of the gaps as memories fade. Plebe Year stories were especially favored.

All service academies put first year students through a grueling, winnowing-out process known as Plebe Year. It begins in July and lasts through the end of the academic year, when the "Firsties" toss hats in the air and leave to take their places in the fleet. At West Point, the summer initiation into military life is known as "beast barracks." At Annapolis, where we are more refined, we simply call it "plebe summer."

Midshipmen learn how to make beds military style, with squared corners and a tautness that will bounce a coin when dropped. We learn to stow our gear with a precision that might seem mindless in the landlubber's roomy environment, but understandable when one considers the cramped space aboard ship. And we learn how to respond to an order: "Aye, aye, Sir."

This year's reunion was especially meaningful for me. Two of my children and three grandchildren were able to join me. Together, we walked the brick sidewalks of Crab Town, as we called Annapolis in my days as a midshipman, and the historic pathways of the Naval Academy yard. We had lunch with 4,000 midshipmen in the largest mess hall in the world. We watching them at parade, as the Naval Academy Band played familiar Sousa marches that stir one's patriotic soul. We saw the Middies whip Delaware at football, extending their record to 7-1, the best football start in 25 years. Nine-year old grandson Jack was duly impressed. As you might imagine, I'm grooming him for a special assignment nine years from now—plebe summer 2013.

* * *

Happy Veterans' Day, dear friends and fellow citizens. On November 11th, please remember those who served their country and those who are still serving their country. We owe our most cherished freedoms to them. And pray that President Bush leads us to a swift and successful conclusion to the war in Iraq.

Chapter 27

This article was my first featured piece in The Record, appearing as the lead in the Sunday Opinion section on January 6, 2002. I had been teaching for two years at three different colleges, and the prevalence of plagiarism was alarming to me. I treated every instance of proven plagiarism seriously, either imposing a failing grade for the paper if the offense was limited to a sentence or two or a failing grade for the course for more extensive violations. One student commented in his end of semester evaluation of the instructor that the thing he liked least about my course was "fear of being executed for plagiarism." A month after my article appeared, The Record wrote an editorial entitled "Cheating by Students" and mentioned my article again.

Making the Grade

—Students plagiarizing best term papers money can buy—

I caught the first two culprits a year ago. I had been teaching only a short while, as an adjunct professor—a fancy name colleges give part-time teachers in lieu of decent pay and benefits. It was near the end of term, and students in my freshman writing class had been assigned a 5-page essay. Two young ladies, both borderline C students, turned in A papers.

At first, I was delighted by what I read. Credit a master teacher at work, I thought. Then I read the papers a second time, focusing on a turn of phrase here, a clever word choice there, writing constructions students rarely use. Suspicious now, I spent the next few hours searching the Internet and, regrettably, found the true sources of both papers. One student had lifted her paper, verbatim, from an obscure article published years earlier. The other student, a bit more industrious, had patched together her paper from several sources. Both passed off another's work as their own. Both flunked the course.

I've read at least a thousand student papers and have acquired, I think, a feel for the way students write. For the most part, they stink. Not all of them. Only about 75%. The reason, of course, is that young people don't read anymore, and their attempts to write a sentence or paragraph show it. Half of them can't identify the subject or verb in a sentence. Try talking about agreement between pronouns and their antecedents, and eyes glaze over. They weren't taught these basic skills in elementary school, or in high school.

But they did learn the art of plagiarism. Why work hours on a paper when one can be generated effortlessly using the Internet? The potential rewards are substantial: better grades; higher class rank; acceptance into a more prestigious college; and, most important for some, parental approval. Chances of getting caught are slim to none. Nobody checks. If by some quirk a student is caught, punishment will be light. Our litigious society has turned school administrators into pusillanimous pushovers.

As a consequence, kids show up at college unprepared to compose a coherent paragraph, but armed with the certain knowledge they can get by their entire academic careers without the need to do so. Students need not rely on their own pilfering skills. There are dozens of dot.coms on the Web advertising research papers for sale. The going rate is about six bucks a page for a canned, prewritten paper, or twenty bucks a page for a custom job.

I typed key words TERM PAPER into my AOL search engine and turned up 32 Web sites of paper mill companies willing to sell me a paper on just about any subject. At Yahoo I found 50 more. Academic publications estimate there are at least 150 companies offering this service. With competition so fierce, companies use catchy names to target customers. For example, the fraternity brothers of "Animal House" fame would undoubtedly be attracted by the paper mill calling itself schoolsucks.com. Those seeking a more professional approach might click on termpapermasters.com or academicpros. com. A more secretive type might choose 007.com.

One company goes after students comfortable with their self-image: lazystudents.com. Need a technical whiz? Go to BigNerds. com. Or, papergeeks.com. "We have no social life," that company boasts. "Let's be frank! All we do is write research papers."

Students in a hurry because they forgot about an assignment due tomorrow can try duenow.com or fastpapers.com. Use a credit card, and a paper can be faxed or e-mailed within an hour. If graduate school admission is a concern and a student needs an A to help her GPA, genius.com is the choice. An A not good enough? Try a-plus-essays.com.

I clicked on speedyresearch.net, which advertised itself as "The Web's Best Source for Term Paper Assistance." I don't doubt the claim. The company provides a search function so students can browse through tens of thousands of term papers in its inventory to find just the right one.

You don't get to read a paper before buying. With clients predisposed to stealing other people's work, that would be economically unwise. But speedyresearch.net does give a brief description, including the number of footnotes, sources cited and pages. The company also rates the proficiency level of its papers, another shopping convenience.

I typed in key word LOVE, clicked the search button, and hit the jackpot—401 papers in inventory, all having something to do with "love." They ranged from a 66-page tome entitled "Analysis of Sex, Love and Death in the Fiction of D.H. Lawrence" to a more modest offering on "Love Canal," the New York hazardous waste site, I presume. The D.H. Lawrence paper was rated "AG", meaning it was "exceptional quality, graduate level." The price? A mere $396, not bad for what obviously would have been several months' work for a student. The Love Canal essay, 9 pages and rated "A", the next lower level, was more affordable at $54.

I thought I'd try another topic and, with tongue planted firmly in cheek, typed in key words ACADEMIC HONESTY. It took just a moment for my electronic helper to report, "No products match your criteria." Paper mill sites all have prominent disclaimers posted on their Web pages—the work, perhaps, of nervous lawyers.

Speedyresearch.net's disclaimer said: "All our materials are sold for research assistance only, not as a finished product for academic credit." Sure. Wink, wink.

Understandably, administrators and professors have become almost fatalistic about plagiarism, but a few are fighting back. According to The Chronicle of Education, Georgetown, Tulane and the University of California are among schools that provide teachers with a service called Turnitin.com. A suspect paper can be scanned into the service, which then searches its own data base and the Internet for the source. Still, some educators feel we may have gone too far in efforts to catch plagiarizers.

In a November 2001 Chronicle article entitled "Forget about Plagiarism. Just Teach," Rebecca Moore Howard, director of the writing program at Syracuse University, warns that "we risk becoming the enemies rather than the mentors of our students; we are replacing the student-teacher relationship with the criminal-police relationship." We teachers need to examine our pedagogy, she suggests. "It is possible students are cheating because they don't value the opportunity of learning in our classes."

Ms. Howard also raises a mirror to a darker side of academia. Who among us, she asks, has not been guilty somewhere in our personal lives of omitting quotation marks, or borrowing a particular useful phrase without attribution?

Indeed, in March 2000 the president of Hastings College retired after being charged with plagiarism. In May 2000 a Duke University freshman researching an English paper caught the president of Wesley College in an act of plagiarism. The college president blamed the error on researchers working for him, but was forced to withdraw his academic paper. In July 2001 Texas A & M fired a professor for plagiarism. In August 2001 Trinity International University fired its law school dean for plagiarizing a law review article.

When our leaders—whether in academia, government, or society in general—engage in shameful conduct and then lie about it, it's not difficult to grasp why appeals to students based on honesty and integrity don't work. But students, adults after all, must themselves bear a measure of responsibility. In a March 1999 plagiarism lecture, Margaret Fain and Peggy Bates of Coastal Carolina University observed that "students have come to college to get a credential—a credential that will allow them to pursue a chosen career. How they get this credential might be less important [to them] than simply getting it."

I'm not one to give up easily, so when this fall semester began, I was determined things would be different, at least in my classes. Yes, I would strive to be the teacher and mentor my students deserved. But I would also insist on honesty in my classroom.

My syllabus for a government and politics class referred to the university handbook, which warns about plagiarism and describes in detail the dire consequences that could result. On the first day of class, I put my own spin on the subject. "Don't do it," I told my students. "If you do it, I'll catch you."

I didn't check their initial assignment closely. It was my first exposure to their writing, and I wanted to give everyone the benefit of the doubt. But while reading their second papers, at mid-term when I knew them better and had an idea what their individual capabilities were, I set aside a half dozen or so that looked suspiciously like plagiarized work. Twenty percent of my class!

I worked the Internet until 3:00 a.m. and tracked down four papers as outright plagiarism, lifted verbatim without attribution. I couldn't find the others, but suspect they were purchased from paper mills. My first inclination was to flunk the four students I had caught red-handed. I spoke to my department head and showed her my proofs. She was supportive, but told me she usually dealt with such matters less harshly, perhaps by failing students for the plagiarized paper, itself, or lowering their final grade in the course. Plagiarism was a reality of contemporary college life, she said. There were software programs designed to detect plagiarism, but no funds in the university budget to purchase them. She didn't elaborate, but I sensed that in the routine weighing of priorities, this university, like many others, had consigned the fight against plagiarism to its wish list. It's a shame, because a well publicized anti-plagiarism tool might have served as an effective deterrent. Speak softly, but carry a big stick.

I met individually with the four students, confronted them with my discovery of their dishonesty, and listened to their profuse apologies. They all came clean, so to speak. Faced with the prospect of suspension or failure for the term, all were close to tears. They begged for a chance to redeem themselves.

In the end, I relented and just failed them for the plagiarized papers, alone. It was, I realized, the practice among my colleagues to handle the problem in this fashion, and I didn't think it would be fair for my plagiarizers to suffer a harsher penalty than the plagiarizers in other classes. If a crackdown is in order, and I believe it is, the university must undertake an institution-wide program to educate faculty and students about plagiarism and, perhaps, to put uniform penalties in place.

Soon after the incident, I did conduct a teach-in with my own students. I wrote truth, honor and integrity on the blackboard and asked, "What do these words mean in today's society?" In the dead silence that followed, I'm sure they were wondering, has Professor Muti taken leave of his senses? What does this have to do with today's lesson? But then tentative hands went up here and there, and we began a period-long discussion of truth, honor and integrity. I eventually guided them to an exploration of their own ethical underpinnings, including the willingness among most students to plagiarize, apparently without the slightest hesitancy. Every one does it, they said. No one seems to be checking, they said, except you.

I talked to them about personal honor, about the bond that should exist between teacher and student. I spoke about how they needed to be honest so their children would be honest. So our society would be honest. I thought I reached a few of them and felt pretty good about the way I handled things. My ego did not remain inflated for long.

Later that week at another university, where my reputation as a hard-nosed teacher is equally well established, I noticed upon entering my classroom that one anonymous disciple of mine had taped a printed sign to the window. In a way, I admired its Hemingwayesque embrace of strong verbs, its eschewal of adjectival modifiers.

"Muty Sucks," it said.

They can't spell either.

Chapter 28

This "In the Arena" column was an adaptation of the "State of the Borough" speech I gave at the 2005 reorganization meeting. Once again, it lays out before the public the dire financial challenges we faced at the local level and my plans to do something about them.

Surviving an Economic "Perfect Storm"

Last week I wrote about what the council and I have been able to accomplish in my first two years. I also promised I would devote the first "In the Arena" column this month to my vision for the future—what do I want to achieve in my final two years as mayor and where do I hope the next mayor will take you.

Let me start with the hard, honest truth about property taxes. Your property taxes will rise every year because the cost of running this town rises every year, and, with very little land remaining for development, we can no longer rely on an expanding tax base to cover the increased costs of doing business. Nor can we count on higher state aid to municipalities; the state's finances are on life support, and we'll be lucky if Trenton doesn't cut back. To survive this economic "perfect storm," we must continue eliminating waste and managing the municipal budget wisely.

There is little we can do to contain costs for certain items: salt for icy roads, utilities, equipment maintenance and replacement, insurance, recycling and garbage collection. Market forces determine the price. Other expenses are beyond our control because the state dictates what we must pay. For example, we will pay about half a million over the next few years to help bail out the state pension system, thanks to imprudent stock investments and borrowing by the Whitman administration. Also, the mandatory property revaluation we went through in 2002-2003 cost us over $400,000, spread out over 5 years.

But the picture is not totally bleak. We can make a significant difference in some areas, like the cost of legal and engineering services. All it takes is a mayor with the chutzpah to impose caps on what professionals can charge and a council willing to follow the mayor's lead, even if he is of the wrong political party.

Because salaries and benefits for borough employees constitute almost two-thirds of our operating budget, that's an area we must concentrate on to put Ramsey on a firm financial footing for the future. You know my thoughts on this subject. I think 90% of you—even my most devoted political opponents—agree with me. Sure, I could cave in to the pressure and allow employees to keep their health insurance unchanged—free family benefits that cost taxpayers $17,000 per employee, increasing by 15-23% a year. Single benefits cost considerably less—*only* $5,000—but the great majority of our employees are on the family plan. We could get by, for another year or two, but it would be irresponsible to take the easy road knowing that in the not too distant future Ramsey's finances would be in dire straits because of it. We've offered a fair compensation package: fair to valued employees, and fair to beleaguered Ramsey taxpayers.

My primary objective, therefore, is to control the controllable expenses as much as possible, while investing money prudently in our future. For the municipal portion of your property taxes, I would consider it a successful outcome if the tax rate were to continue on a steady, *gradual* incline, rising each year at or near the rate of inflation, but no more. We've been able to achieve that in 2003 and 2004 with increases under 3% both years, thanks partly to cost cutting initiatives and partly to a surplus I inherited. The surplus allows us time to bring expenses under better control, but it will be used up in another year or two—good reason why salaries and benefits have to be addressed now, not later.

My fervor for controlling expenses doesn't mean I am against spending tax dollars for worthwhile projects. We cannot take a head-in-the-sand, Ostrich approach to providing for our future needs. The longer we postpone necessary capital investments, the more costly those improvements will be. Insuring that Ramsey has a sufficient water supply, for example, will require a sizeable capital outlay, but we have no choice. Water is a basic need. Other projects, like upgrading Finch Park or finally getting started on the downtown beautification, may not be life sustaining; nevertheless, they, too, are essential if we are to maintain the quality of life we expect as citizens of Ramsey. We can afford to do these projects if we follow sound financial practices.

Sometimes we can obtain facilities or make improvements at little or no cost. We recently took title to a new lighted playing field. The developer of the active adult community on the east side of Route 17 donated the land and constructed the field, primarily because of the planning board's careful shepherding of the project through the approval process. Working quietly behind the scenes, we got an outstanding facility for our town at no cost to taxpayers. The adult complex, itself, is a grand slam, in that it will add over $50 million in ratables to our tax base with no effect on our schools. The units will have deed restrictions to prohibit school age children from residing there.

Curbs and sidewalks on Wyckoff Avenue will finally be repaired this spring, once again at little or no cost to taxpayers because of a special state grant. We'll be seeking grants for other projects, like the Finch Park upgrade. Finishing touches on phase 1 of the Finch Park rejuvenation will take place soon. When the expanded parking lot is paved and tree and flower plantings take root this spring, 70 parking spaces will have been added in a beautiful setting. We may be able to eliminate street parking on Church Street, always a problematic safety issue. It may also give us space for a bicycle lane on Church and Island Road, an idea advanced by residents Joe Carey and Jim Dolan. Both Joe and Jim have volunteered countless hours to help us deal with traffic and pedestrian safety issues in town. A modest building renovation for seniors' use will also be completed soon, giving them a safe place to hold meetings and activities, all on one floor with plenty of parking.

Phases 2 and 3 of the Finch Park project are still under consideration, and the Ramsey Recreation Commission, under the able leadership of Chairman Joe Palmer, is coordinating those efforts. We are also thinking about a band shell for the numerous concerts that take place in the park, perhaps with corporate sponsorship to lower cost to taxpayers. A walking path, circumventing the entire park, is another feature that shouldn't cost much. There is grant money out there for park facilities, and we'll apply for as much as possible.

The downtown business district facelift was conceived of during the prior administration, and I fully support its implementation. The first phase will finally get underway this summer. It extends from Central Avenue to Spruce Street and includes lots of off-street parking to supplement the existing spaces on Main Street. We've got an ordinance in the works that will give the Design Review Board more teeth in controlling the appearance of business signs, helping to create a better look for downtown. A strong, vibrant commercial district is essential to any community. We've already started that effort with NJ Transit paying the entire cost of the downtown train station restoration, now completed. Ramsey's downtown will be second to none in our area when we get through, once again with a very small investment by taxpayers. We get back this investment because when businesses on Main Street prosper, landlords can charge higher rents. When rents go up, property values go up, and with rising property values for commercial real estate, the burden on residential real estate is eased.

In addition to recreational facilities, we must attend to serious drainage problems in many sections of our town. Residents on DeBaun Avenue, North Island Avenue, the west side of Church Street, and six or eight other areas have been plagued with flooding problems just about every time we have a strong downpour. This has been going on for decades, and it is time we did something about it.

We will do all these capital projects economically, without any appreciable effect on the municipal tax rate, by the judicious use of bonding. We can get much done now, while interest rates are low, and still retire all our debt within 12 years. I will be working this year with the council, along with the entire Citizens Budget Advisory Task Force, to formalize a plan to do just that.

As much as we try to manage things better at the municipal level, you mustn't forget that the mayor and council control just 23% of your property tax bill. County taxes comprise about 10%, and the portion that goes to support Ramsey public schools is about 67%. When the full impact of school construction bonds kicks in this tax year, that proportion will likely increase.

I know I've been outspoken on school finances, but, to be fair, the Board of Education copes with problems even more onerous than those we face in municipal government. Unfunded state and federal mandates make up much of its budget; consequently, it must look to Trenton and Washington for some, but not all of the solution to the problem. The Ramsey BOE has been in the forefront of the debate over fairness in public education funding. Nevertheless, we cannot rely on the hope that legislators will do the right thing. There is a significant element that is controllable at the local level, and it demands attention.

Salaries and benefits make up the bulk of the school budget, just as they do in the municipal budget. To the extent that it has the will, the BOE can begin the process of bringing that line item under control, but it will be difficult. The New Jersey Education Association is the most formidable union in the state. Legislators, in an effort to curry favor with teachers and their union, have enacted laws that prevent local school boards from negotiating effectively. To make matters worse, there is always the risk that teachers might use students as pawns in the struggle for a contract to their liking. It happened three years ago in Ridgewood, that bastion of gentility in Bergen County. The Ridgewood BOE was trying to trim back on health benefits, but backed down when teachers began taking it out on the kids. When one school board succumbs to the pressure, raising salaries far above the inflation rate and doing nothing to curtail benefits, teachers in neighboring towns then point to that particular result, which becomes the prevailing standard for contract settlements. And state officials usually back them up. It's a vicious cycle, and one of these days, a brave Board of Education will say, "Enough." I hope that school board will be Ramsey's.

Another objective, then, is to explore with the Ramsey Board of Education ways in which we might help each other save taxpayers' money. There must be missed opportunities out there, some stones we have left unturned. Can we share personnel, equipment, or services? For example, do both the town and the BOE have to maintain separate buildings and grounds departments, or can we save money by having one department service municipal and school needs alike? Can we get lower insurance rates if we work together? Can students earn academic credit by interning in municipal offices, thereby saving labor costs? I don't know the answers to any of these questions. I don't even know all the questions. It is clear, however, that we have to find ways to do things better.

Toward that end, I announced at the January 2nd council reorganization meeting my idea of a joint committee of council members and school board members, the only function of which will be to identify ways in which the Borough and the school board can work together for the benefit of all Ramsey residents. If the BOE finds the idea meritorious, I will appoint three council members to join with three BOE members. With the professional advice of the superintendent of schools and borough administrator, they will meet regularly with no preconceived agenda other than to save tax dollars. I am not aware of any such committee in the State of New Jersey, but so what. Someone has to take the lead in these things, if we are ever to find workable solutions. Why not Ramsey?

Chapter 29

"Here's Looking at You, Kid"

We've had a couple of successful family movie nights in Finch Park. Outdoor movies are always at the mercy of weather, of course, but so far we've been lucky in that regard.

Later this month, the Ramsey Recreation Commission will sponsor a movie in the park for us old timers. The August 28th event has been dubbed "Burgers and Bogie" and will feature one of the all-time great Humphrey Bogart movies—"Casablanca"—and free hamburgers and soda. Volunteers from the Ramsey Junior Football League will do the food service. Donations to this fine organization will be gratefully accepted, but don't feel obligated. This is to be a free evening of entertainment in honor of Ramsey's seniors. Everyone who loves a good movie is welcome. If you like the idea, maybe we'll have a Bogie night next year, too. "The Maltese Falcon" (*"It's the stuff dreams are made of"*) and "Treasure of the Sierra Madre" (*"Badges? We don' need no stinkin' badges"*) come to mind as possibilities.

I love movies, but hardly ever *go* to the movies. My taste, you see, runs to the old flicks—mostly black and white classics from the Forties and Fifties, with a few from the Thirties and Sixties making the grade. The other night I sat down and pondered my top ten favorites. By the time I was finished, I had 22 titles on my list. These are movies I always watch whenever they are shown on television.

I've seen these films so often that I know most of the dialogue before it's spoken. *"It wuz you, Charlie. You said, 'Kid, tonight's not your night. We're going for the price on Wilson.' Not my night? I coulda taken that bum apart. Instead, he gets a title shot in the ballpark and I get a one-way ticket to Palookaville."* (Marlon Brando, "On the Waterfront.")

Fortunately for my wife, who doesn't share this passion for ancient Hollywood and who looks askance at me when I blurt out an actor's lines in advance, most of the films I like are on late, after she's gone to bed. She tolerates one line, however, that just happens to be from "Casablanca." Years ago, while a string quartet played Ravel's "Bolero," I proposed to her during a romantic cruise on the River Seine. Now, when Humphrey looks into Ingrid's eyes and I say with a bad imitation of Bogie's lisp, *"We'll always have Paris,"* she smiles.

But usually it is just Chelsea the Wonder Dog, First Dog of Ramsey, and I who watch our old movies together in the wee small hours. She wags appreciatively at each utterance from her master. (I'm not sure if the pretzel or potato chip snacks have anything to do with the wags.) We've put our heads together and pared down the list of favorites to these top ten. Let us know what you think. If you can name three stars in each movie without looking them up, Chelsea will do one of her famous tricks for you and I'll cut your property taxes.

1. On the Waterfront
2. Twelve O'Clock High
3. Casablanca
4. High Noon
5. A Man for All Seasons
6. From Here to Eternity
7. To Kill a Mockingbird
8. Shane
9. The Grapes of Wrath
10. Gunga Din

I think that last movie, "Gunga Din," is based on a Rudyard Kipling poem. I had thought about putting another Kipling-inspired movie on the list, but omitted it for fear of providing more grist for the never-say-die "recall Mayor Muti" mill. It's a movie from the Seventies, starring Sean Connery and Michael Caine as two fortune-seeking veterans of the British army in 19th-century India. They cross the Hindu Kush on foot, organize and train a native army, and conquer Kafirastan.

The name of the movie? "The Man Who Would Be King."

Chapter 30

Making Public Policy—A Case History

On May 26th the Ramsey Borough Council introduced by unanimous vote an ordinance to establish guidelines for videotaping and audio taping public meetings. A public hearing is scheduled for June 9th.

This particular ordinance has generated controversy. Some have called it an infringement of the public's right to access information about its government. The borough council and I don't agree with that view and are certainly interested in hearing from you on the issue. But please, read the ordinance for yourselves; don't rely on how others may characterize it. E-mail me (mayormuti@ramseynj.com) and I'll send you a copy. If you cannot attend the June 9th public hearing, you can also e-mail your comments to me and I will make sure my colleagues on the council receive them.

It is important not only to read the actual policy document, but also to understand the context in which it was created: the *how* and *why* of making this public policy.

Most policy initiatives are in response to a problem, and that is clearly what happened in this case. A resident notified the borough clerk that he intended to videotape council meetings for later broadcast on his private web site. At first, one might say, "so what." It's a public meeting, so why can't you capture everything that happens on videotape and show it to the world.

The answer, I suppose, is that it is a dangerous world, and some things that happen at council meetings involve children.

From time to time, children come before the governing body to receive recognition for athletic or other achievements. Cub scouts sometimes participate in meetings as a way to enhance their understanding of civic functions and government. The names of these children are announced at the meetings.

It was the considered judgment of the governing body that videotaping such children and then showing the videotapes on a web site or other means of broadcast would pose a potential danger to the children.

I have nineteen years experience as a prosecutor, so perhaps I have been exposed to this area more than most members of the public. But I didn't rely solely on my own sense of the risk involved. I consulted with our police chief and with detectives who are experts in the field, including one from the computer crimes unit of the Bergen County Prosecutor's Office. The experts strongly agreed that videotaping children, identifying the children by name, and then broadcasting those images on the Internet should be strictly prohibited. "Without question," one of them told me.

We asked the borough attorney to research this issue. Did we have the right to place restrictions on the videotaping of public meetings? Could we legally tell this resident to shut down his video camera when children were participating in the meeting.

The answer was "no", we could not limit things because we did not have a policy in place. New Jersey case law clearly required public bodies to enact written policies on the subject of audio taping and videotaping their meetings, if those bodies wanted to exercise any control over the process. And those legal cases were 20 years old, decided before the invention of the Internet. No New Jersey court had even considered the consequences of the situation we feared most—broadcasting the images and names of kids over the Internet.

Ironically, the New Jersey legislature did consider this issue, but only with regard to Boards of Education. State law prohibits school boards from showing the images of children with identifying information (like names) on their web sites without parental consent. The legislature neglected, however, to prohibit such conduct outside the school board context.

One might ask, "Why not just work things out with the man who wanted to videotape the meetings? Surely he would be reasonable and agree to turn off the video cameras while children were participating in the meetings." One would think so, but in this particular case, we had information that led us to conclude otherwise.

This same person had also begun to videotape Board of Education meetings. At one recent BOE meeting, the board president asked the man to refrain from videotaping children who were participating. He refused. Only when the board president threatened to call police did the man shut off his camera. Clearly, we could not rely on appeals to reason with this individual. We needed a written policy—one that was comprehensive enough to deal with contingencies. And we had to act quickly. We had 30 junior cheerleaders scheduled to attend the April 28th council meeting to receive awards.

The borough attorney and I researched the case law further and got help from the NJ League of Municipalities. Together, we drafted a policy and sent it home to council members on April 9th for their review. The council adopted the policy unanimously at our April 14th meeting, so that it would be in place for April 28th. (The cheerleaders later rescheduled their appearance for the second meeting in May.) The policy was adopted with the express understanding that it would undergo later refinements and be reintroduced as an ordinance with input from the public.

And that is exactly what happened. The proposed ordinance introduced on May 26th sets reasonable guidelines for audio taping and videotaping public meetings. It follows recommended procedures established by court cases, the NJ Supreme Court, and New York State courts. Indeed, it is more lenient in most respects than the court guidelines.

The borough council and I are committed to conducting the public's business openly, except when the public interest might be harmed. Some subjects must be discussed in closed session—personnel matters, contract negotiations, real estate purchases, and litigation, for example—under New Jersey law, until the matters are concluded. There is a need, also, for reasonable restrictions on audio taping and videotaping public meetings. Children at those meetings must be protected, and the meetings must proceed without undue interruptions or distractions. I think we achieved the right balance with this proposed ordinance, but would appreciate your views.

Chapter 31

Another Op-Ed piece in The Record. This one was published on October 10, 2005, about the time two vacancies arose on the U. S. Supreme Court.

The Founding Fathers—
Fabled but Fallible Framers of the U.S. Constitution

President George W. Bush says he will nominate only "strict constructionists" to the Supreme Court, meaning he wants justices who will interpret the U.S. Constitution as the Framers intended. Chief Justice John Roberts, his first appointee, and now Harriet Miers, his choice to replace Justice Sandra Day O'Connor, both appear to meet that test, although nervous Nellies on the far-right are afraid of being "Soutered" once again. Justice David Souter, a 1990 appointment of Bush Senior, had impeccable Conservative credentials, too. But once ensconced on the Court, the New Hampshire Republican has tended to think for himself and not conform to anyone's preconception of his judicial bent. His name has come to represent every Conservative's worst nightmare: a tenured-for-life judge, assumed to be one of their own, who turns out to be, gasp, a Liberal!

It has become something of a mantra, this strict constructionism, as though the 55 men who gathered in Philadelphia that sultry summer of 1787 to draft the U.S. Constitution, the "Framers," were prescient super-beings. No, they weren't able to leap tall buildings in a single bound; but if President Bush, the Federalist Society, and every Rush Limbaugh-like talk show host are to be credited, these gentlemen defied not gravity but time itself. They've transcended their 18th century domain and speak to us now, more than two centuries later, like oracles.

No one loves the Constitution more than I. I have studied it for 30 years and have taught it to college students for four years. It is truly a remarkable document, the oldest written constitution in the world. After the first ten amendments, the Bill of Rights, were ratified in 1791, the Constitution has been amended just 17 more times. But were the Framers infallible? Do their words rise to the level of divine revelation? Can we impute to them an ability to foretell the future? Decidedly not.

These were 55 elite members of their society, all well read and highly intelligent. But I think they would be shocked, and probably amused, to know their political descendants, living in a complex world barely imaginable 218 years ago, were hanging on their every word.

In fact, the Framers, almost one-third of them slave owners, made serious misjudgments, not the least of which was their failure to address the rights of half the populace. At the Second Continental Congress in 1776, John Adams received a letter from wife Abigail. "Don't forget the ladies," she admonished Adams, as he and Jefferson worked on the Declaration of Independence. But, indeed, they forgot the ladies then and the Framers forgot them later. Without a Constitutional right to vote, women were barred from the political process and relegated to second class citizenship. Not until the Nineteenth Amendment was ratified in 1920 did that begin to change.

Other segments of American society fared worse. To keep the South as participants in the nation-building experiment, slavery, though not mentioned by name anywhere in the Constitution, not only was condoned, it was allowed to flourish. Plantation owners were given a 20-year green light to import all the slaves they needed. Slaves were property and had no rights. In fact, they weren't even counted as full human beings. In perhaps the most shameful chapter in Constitutional history, something historians refer to as the Three-Fifths Compromise, a slave was to be counted both for representation and taxation purposes as three-fifths of a "whole person."

One might argue that we should cut the Framers a little slack. Slavery and male domination of the political process were facts of life in the 18th century, and these men, after all, were creatures of their times. Just so. But those who would make that argument cannot have it both ways. Men locked into the mindset of their own era do not become oracles of another era.

If you think I still have not made my case, dear reader, I have two words that will carry the day. As you read them, you will nod your head vigorously and say, "You know, he's right—the Framers did make mistakes." Here are the two words: *Electoral College.*

In what must be the most convoluted scheme ever devised by men to choose their leader, the Framers came up with the cockamamie idea of the Electoral College to choose presidents. Why? Because they didn't trust us to elect a chief executive. They thought of the American public—"the masses"—as being mostly uninformed, ruled by emotions, and easily swayed by appeals to their baser instincts. The selection of a president couldn't be left to such an unruly bunch; rather, it would fall to a layer of elite citizens, just like the Framers, to make that choice.

Electors were to be chosen in a manner determined by state legislatures and in numbers equal to the Congressional representation of each state. The electors would gather at a time and place designated by Congress, and each would cast two votes. The candidate with the highest vote total, provided it was a majority, would become president; the candidate with the second highest vote total would become vice president. If there was a tie or no one received a majority, the election would be thrown into the House of Representatives for a final decision.

This brainchild of the Framers lasted just 12 years before it broke down, threatening the very existence of the American republic.

President John Adams was seeking reelection in 1800 as the candidate of the Federalist Party. Thomas Jefferson was the presidential candidate of the Democratic-Republican Party. His running mate was Aaron Burr, a man of unparalleled ambition and a participant just a few years later in the most famous duel in American history. Every Democratic-Republican elector dutifully cast his two votes, one for Jefferson and one for Burr, and those two men tied for first place. The election went to the House for resolution, as the Framers had prescribed.

Burr was expected to defer to Jefferson, but refused to step aside. Instead, he tried to get lame-duck Federalist representatives to support him for president. Jefferson eventually prevailed, but not without delay, uncertainty, and turmoil. The Twelfth Amendment fixed that immediate anomaly in 1804; thereafter, electors would cast one vote for president and one separate vote for vice president.

The problem was that the Framers didn't foresee the development of partisan party politics. When George Washington was elected unanimously by the first electors, the only president to achieve that distinction, political parties didn't exist. The Framers believed that would be the permanent condition of the American democracy: reasonable men gathering every four years to choose the best man to lead the country and reaching that conclusion by consensus. They couldn't have been more wrong. Modern-day Americans, observers of the constant bickering and sporadic nastiness between Republicans and Democrats, harbor no such illusions.

Despite changes to the Electoral College system in 1804, the presidential election of 1824 was once again decided in the House of Representatives. On three other occasions, the popular vote winner in November went on to lose the presidency in December in the Electoral College, most recently in 2000 when Gore received a half million more votes than Bush. A handful of other elections were so close they almost ended the same way.

As you might have surmised by now, I am not a strict constructionist. Nevertheless, I revere the Constitution as the grandest "blueprint for government" ever devised by Man and honor the men who wrote it for their wisdom in knowing what they could do and what they could not do in Philadelphia that summer of 1787. The Constitution is to be admired as much for its purposeful ambiguities and generalities as for its more precise provisions.

It was and is a "living" Constitution—legal scholars and justices of the Supreme Court have characterized it as such—to be interpreted according to "evolving community standards." Justice William J. Brennan, Jr., put it this way: "The genius of the Constitution rests not in any static meaning it might have had in a world that is dead and gone, but in the adaptability of its great principles to cope with current problems and current needs." Our grandchildren's grandchildren, a hundred years from now, will have the same flexibility to deal with problems they face. I hope, also, they have the same love for the document that gives them that power.

Chapter 32

Richard J. Codey, A Man for All Seasons

I was disappointed when Democratic State Senate Majority Leader Richard J. Codey opted out of the governor's race with Jon Corzine, primarily because of Corzine's unlimited personal war chest of campaign funds. Codey had served with distinction as interim governor after McGreevey's resignation, surprising many with his candor and political acumen. These next two pieces appeared as "In the Arena" columns, in praise of one Trenton politician I truly like.

Run Dick Run

How does an honest, plain-vanilla public servant like Richard J. Codey, a family man of modest means who would rather coach his kid's basketball team than cozy up to fat cats at a fund-raiser—how does a guy like that stand a chance? The answer, apparently, is that he does not.

Early last week, Acting Governor Dick Codey opted out of what promised to be a spirited and close race with US Sen. Jon Corzine for the Democratic gubernatorial nomination. The decision saddened me, not just because Codey represented everything that is decent and good in an elected official, but also because it was a reaffirmation of the sleazy, all-powerful influence of money in NJ politics.

Corzine spent $63 million in his senate campaign four years ago, using mostly his own fortune and outspending his Republican opponent Bob Franks by 10 to 1. He just squeaked by Franks in the vote count. The senator could easily commit twice that amount to his race for governor—that's "walking around" money for him—a fact not lost on Codey or the party bosses. Democratic organizations from Bergen to Mercer to the southern tier were climbing all over themselves to board the Corzine steamroller. And why not? The man is an attractive candidate not just for his personal wealth, but also for his reputation as a capable and likeable person.

Codey, on the other hand, had not endeared himself to party bosses. He's far too independent to suit those practitioners of backroom politics. And far too principled. That's where a winning strategy could have worked, in my mind.

I would have proposed that Governor Codey take a fresh approach, that he position himself as the un-Cola, the anti-politician politician, the candidate who is his own man—bought by no one, owned by no one, beholden to no one.

Codey was already halfway there. Newspaper reporters, anesthetized by years of covering the usual suspects in Trenton, love him. He is Everyman. The guy next door who, thrust into the spotlight by fate, rises almost Truman-like to the occasion. I don't have access to polling information, but I'd guess Codey's positives are very high, considering the short time he's been governor.

The reason for Codey's popularity? His candor. I think the public is finally ready for a government official willing to speak the truth, even when it comes with political risk. Not easily digestible, feel-good truths, but hard truths like those contained in this speech I prepared, unsoliticted, for Codey's announcement of his candidacy.

Dear friends and fellow citizens. New Jersey is once again in financial crisis, facing yet another multi-billion budget deficit because we politicians have failed to level with the people of New Jersey. We have not followed a sound financial plan. Year after year, we have avoided making difficult choices, afraid the opposing party would try to capitalize on any attempt to realistically deal with our problems. As a consequence, the problems not only remain but are getting worse. When we spoke to the public, we followed the "Mary Poppins" formula: "A spoonful of sugar makes the medicine go down." But in our actions, we gave you too much sugar and not enough medicine. In other words, we didn't trust you enough. We didn't think you could handle the truth.

I was as guilty of that mindset as every other legislator. But today, as I announce my candidacy for governor of New Jersey, I promise that things will be different. I will start by telling you there is no such thing as a free lunch.

In the coming months, I hope by my candor and job performance to earn your trust and your votes. I can't compete with the millions my opponent will throw into this race for governor, so you will have to pay close attention to what I say and do. Forget the 30-second sound bites on television and the slick mail pieces you will be inundated with—I can't afford any of that stuff. What I can do is the job the State Constitution has entrusted me with. For the next 11 months, I will work hard at being your governor, someone you can trust to tell you the truth about every issue, whether you like it or not. I will hold frequent press conferences, so reporters can put me to the test. I will let you know what I think about every problem we face. I won't duck anything. And I won't spend time campaigning, except for the last six weeks before the primary and the last four weeks before the general election. Then, I'll hit the road, visiting every one of New Jersey's 566 towns, villages, boroughs, and cities, listening to what you have to say.

Unfortunately, Governor Codey did not consult me before deciding to withdraw from contention. I predict we'll regret his decision not to seek a full term on his own. He's a good man.

Governor Dick Codey Continues to Impress

If you missed the budget message Governor Dick Codey delivered to a joint session of the state legislature on March 1st, you missed something truly special. I don't know if I've ever heard as fine a speech, both in style and substance, by a New Jersey public official in my lifetime. No, I am not laying it on too thick. This guy is amazing.

For the first time, we heard the truth about state finances. Codey spoke plainly and clearly: "The practice of spending like there's no tomorrow ends today." He laid out an austere budget for 2006, one that hurts every constituency a little bit, but is absolutely necessary if we are to survive this crisis.

"The good news is we're not bankrupt," the governor said. "The bad news is, we're close."

Perhaps the most statesmanlike aspect of the speech was the governor's refusal to point a partisan finger at anyone, while laying the blame on everyone in the legislative chamber, himself included. "Fiscal gimmicks and borrowing have been a bipartisan budget addiction," he said. "Both parties have borrowed recklessly and spent well beyond the state's means."

Indeed, under former Governor Whitman and a Republican controlled legislature for most of her almost eight years in office, state spending increased more than 50%. Yes, she cut taxes, but financed her spending spree by quadrupling state debt, from $4 billion to almost $16 billion. When the economy tanked in 2001, McGreevey faced multi-billion dollar deficits for his first three budget cycles, but then he and the Democratic controlled legislature also succumbed to the siren song of credit card spending.

Last year, on a challenge led by State Senator Leonard Lance, Republican minority leader, the NJ Supreme Court finally put a stop to the practice of borrowing to meet operating expenses.

Codey pointed out that about 75% of the $27.3 billion budget merely passes through state hands before it is directed out of the treasury either by fixed costs or by property tax relief programs, like aid to municipalities and school districts. It costs $2 billion for debt service and $3 billion for federally mandated Medicaid costs, for example—things we have no control over. Court ordered funding for Abbott district schools eats up half of the aid to public education.

When we finally get to the 25% of "controllable" expenses, items like the runaway costs of providing health insurance for state employees and retired teachers and other state workers allow little flexibility.

Perhaps the most controversial budget proposal is Codey's plan to eliminate the NJ Saver program of tax rebates for most New Jerseyans. He keeps reduced rebates for seniors and the disabled. This particular measure saves $1 billion. Codey says he is willing to listen to any reasonable alternatives, but points out that attacks on his proposal should be accompanied by specific alternatives. In other words, if you object to the elimination of the NJ Saver rebates, specify what 'revenue generators' (a euphemism for *taxes*) or program cuts you will recommend to make up the $1 billion shortfall.

Those who shout out buzz words like "eliminate waste" need to recognize that the costs of operating state government in Trenton amount to just $1.3 billion out of a total budget of $27.4 billion. Not much room. Still, Codey's budget reduces the state work force by 500 jobs, entirely by attrition. He has imposed a 10% decrease in the spending of every department.

There will be those who go on the partisan attack. That is the nature of politics, I guess. As Governor Codey put it, this type of criticism amounts to "unrealistic sound bites by those who don't have the responsibility to govern."

Once again, Senator Leonard Lance, the Republican minority leader, sounded a high note in reaction to Codey's speech. "It was a somber and serious speech," he said. "The day of reckoning is at hand." Lance is right. With leaders like him and Codey, I feel hopeful.

The governor put it perfectly in his speech: "Now is the time for leadership, not showmanship."

Chapter 33

Another "In the Arena" column, my next to last.

Reflections on a National Day of Prayer

I am not religious, despite my brief stint as an altar boy in old St. Paul's on Cherry Lane, the church my grandparents worshipped in almost a hundred years ago. I say "brief" because Latin did not flow trippingly from my tongue back then (it was before Miss Preische got hold of me at Ramsey High), and I was soon banished by the good sisters. Nevertheless, I enjoy a first-class religious service of any denomination, especially those graced by rousing hymns and sermons that inspire us to be better human beings.

Two weeks ago, I had the great privilege to be present for ecumenical services at Church of the Redeemer. The occasion was the 54th National Day of Prayer, a tradition started by President Harry Truman and carried forward by every president since.

I am uncomfortable with the way many politicians today pointedly display their religious faith at every conceivable opportunity. It's wonderful they find such strength in it, but I prefer my politics a bit more secular. So when the Rev. Dr. Carol Brighton, pastor at Church of the Redeemer, welcomed the congregation by saying she, too, was not a big fan of government getting involved with religion, I almost signed up to be a Lutheran, right on the spot. I like a religious leader who values the separation of church and state. As Dr. Brighton said, that's the only way we can preserve our religious freedoms.

The Community Prayer Service was well attended, and I hope

by writing about it, I can encourage more folks to participate next year on the first Thursday in May.

Councilman Jeff Heller wrote a beautiful "Prayer for our Nation" and delivered it most impressively. Others offered prayers for our leaders, families, children and youth, and senior citizens. Rev. Michael Carrier, pastor of the First Presbyterian Church, prayed for our churches and synagogues. Two well spoken Ramsey High students, recited prayers for our schools and for peace. A woman, whose son is in the Navy, read a "Prayer for the Military" and named Ramsey residents who are currently serving. Then, VFW Post Commander Guy Green, a Naval Reservist just back from the Middle East, and Navy Petty Officer Andy Gamble demonstrated the folding of our nation's flag as Marine Matt Soldano, an Iraq War veteran, narrated the significance of each fold.

Guarantees of religious freedom are among the most important of our civil liberties. I've read too much history of atrocities committed by adherents of one religion against those of another to treat such freedoms lightly. Yet, I see no harm in invoking the name of God in our motto, in our pledge to the flag, and on other occasions of state. When the Framers of the U.S. Constitution wrote in the First Amendment, "Congress shall make no law respecting the establishment of religion," I don't think they meant to banish all mention of God. Indeed, if you read the Declaration of Independence, you will find four references to a Supreme Being. Even Jefferson, its principal author and the least religious of our presidents, saw merit in such acknowledgment.

We *can* keep church and state separate and have done so successfully for two centuries. But when on May 5th those of us at the Community Prayer Service sang, "America, America, God shed his grace on thee," and when we all sang, "God bless America, land that I love, stand beside her and guide her through the night with a light from above," I felt great pride in this wonderful nation of ours.

This is a stressful time for the United States of America—a time, perhaps, to recall the words of Stephen Decatur, one of our great naval heroes.

"My country," he said, raising his glass in a toast, "in her commerce with other nations may she always be in the right, but, right or wrong, my country."

Chapter 34

Reorganization Meeting Speech—2004

Ladies and Gentlemen, thank you for attending this reorganization of Ramsey government. I congratulate my colleagues Dave Bisaillon and Chris Botta on their reelection and swearing in today. I also congratulate Howard Cantor on his election as Council President. I fully expect to work well with Howard in the same spirit of cooperation that I enjoyed with Dave Bisaillon last year.

Of course, cooperation does not mean full agreement all the time. If that were so, you wouldn't be getting your money's worth because there would be no testing of ideas, no reconsideration of past practices, no likelihood of improvement.

When we members of the governing body disagree on policy issues, we need to make sure that our debate on those issues is an honest one, not one conducted with superficial applause lines to evoke an emotional reaction from the public.

I hope that minds are not already made up as to the direction we take in 2004, without benefit of information that has yet to be compiled or recommendations from our borough professionals, members of the Citizens' Budget Advisory Task Force, and leaders of emergency services organizations and other units. It would be the height of irresponsibility, I think, for government leaders to take some blood oath – like "READ MY LIPS—NO NEW TAXES" – without knowing fully what our needs are, what opportunities there may be to cut costs, and what other revenues we might expect.

We will be faced with great challenges this year, not the least of which is the budget and property taxes. How we meet those challenges is yet to be determined, but I have every hope it will be with leadership, political courage and wisdom.

Chapter 35

A Bit Too Cocksure for my Own Good

"In the Arena," January 7, 2004

I began fairly brimming with ideas and ideals, but perhaps a bit too cocksure for my own good. Yes, I had been elected mayor with 62% of the vote in a huge turnout. But I soon learned that criticism comes easy; it is much more difficult to govern. The hard part was about to begin.

The 2003 municipal budget required immediate attention, but other problems loomed: negotiations with five employee unions whose contracts expired the day I took office, the first property revaluation in over ten years, and the largest jump in the cost of employee health benefits in probably the last 20 years, to name a few. Fortunately, I had a borough council I could work with. Despite differences you may have read about in the newspapers, I think we agreed 90% of the time.

Under our borough form of government, the mayor has little power when it comes to the municipal budget and setting the tax rate. If the council passes a budget I don't agree with, I cannot veto it. (Budgets are passed by resolution, not ordinance.) Nevertheless, I can try to persuade, to lead the council in the right direction. That's what occurred in 2003.

I spent many hours trying to figure a way to reduce the tax rate, while at the same time maintain services and protect our financial future. The borough administrator, chief financial officer and auditor assisted me in that attempt and reached the same conclusion I did.

The council's Finance and Administration Committee went through a similar exercise under the leadership of Councilman Botta. But the numbers were bleak. Over a million less in surplus from the prior year, hundreds of thousands less in anticipated interest income, hundreds of thousands more for insurance benefits, a half million more in state pension contributions in the next few years, uncertainty regarding open labor contracts and future state aid, and so on.

We could have reduced the tax rate by using more retained surplus, but every model I ran showed us paying the piper with double-digit tax rate increases three years out. We couldn't count on the state suddenly regaining its financial health, so we chose the unpopular but prudent course, rather than the politically expedient one.

It was I who proposed that we raise the municipal tax rate 2%, and after careful consideration, the council backed me by a 4-2 vote. Furthermore, eight members of the Citizens' Budget Advisory Task Force and six members of the Board of Public Works—all originally appointed by former mayor Scerbo—agreed with the new approach we were to take in 2003.

For most of you, that meant about a $40 increase in the municipal share of your property taxes. Any larger increase you may have experienced was caused by school taxes and the property revaluation. (Of course, neither the council nor I had any control over those two factors.) If we're fortunate, you'll see another $40 increase in 2004, and $40 in 2005, and $40 the year after that. You get the idea—small, incremental increases at or near the rate of inflation, while we do everything we can to improve municipal services, eliminate waste, and control expenses.

The council will be under political pressure to not raise the tax rate in 2004—to pretend that the cost of operating your municipal government is not going up. Like the ostrich, they will likely see the temporary benefit of burying one's head in the sand. I'm counting on them to resist that urge and believe they will do the right thing for Ramsey in the end.

We must also face up to another unpleasant task in 2004—reducing by a significant amount the health insurance benefits of borough employees. It will be a challenge. Our employees—hard-working folks with families to support—are understandably sensitive to the subject of pay and benefits, but we have no choice but to address it. (Police officers did agree to a change in health insurance benefits that will save taxpayers over $100,000 in 2004 and every year thereafter, and for that I am grateful and proud of them.)

Right now, all full-time employees and their eligible dependents get free health insurance. "Full time" means a 20-hour work week, but the council seems willing to accept my suggestion that we make 35 hours per week the standard for health benefits eligibility. (We don't have many 20-hour employees getting benefits.) We give employees a generous Blue Cross/Blue Shield package that includes 100% coverage in network (with hundreds of doctors and health care providers to choose from), 80% out of network and a prescription drug benefit. After the first $5,000 in medical expenses, we provide 100% coverage whether in or out of network. There is a $200 deductible, with a maximum of two deductibles per family.

The cost to the borough for family plan coverage is over $12,000 per employee per year. Single coverage is less, of course. But in either case, the employee contributes nothing. The total cost of medical insurance benefits for borough employees in 2003 was about $1,321,000, up 23.1% over 2002. Add the free dental benefit, and we're up around $1,426,000. We experienced double-digit increases in 2002 and 2001, too, and have a letter from our insurance carrier setting the projected increase at 19% for 2004. If we do nothing to reduce coverage, that means we'll approach $1.75 million in 2004, $2 million in 2005, and $2.5 million in 2006. The longer we wait to address the problem, the harder it will be on taxpayers and employees.

I hope you agree that we must take action now. Whatever your opinion, though, do yourself a favor as a taxpayer and write a letter during the next few weeks to the Mayor and Council at 33 N. Central Avenue, or send an e-mail to mayormuti@ramseynj.com. Tell us what you think about this issue or any other issue. I'll pass on all communications, pro and con, to the council. You can be sure we read every letter we get from residents. Please give your name and address—a letter is much more effective if the writer has the courage to take a stand while letting his or her identity be known.

Happy New Year dear friends and fellow citizens of Ramsey. I'll try to do better in 2004.

Chapter 36

At the 2005 reorganization meeting, I began the practice of calling the mayor's speech the "State of the Borough" address, taking a page, of course, from our governor's "State of the State" speech each year, and the president's "State of the Union" address. I followed that concept in 2006, and, I'm happy to say, the new mayor continued it in 2007. It's become a tradition, I suppose.

This speech was delivered at what turned out to be my last reorganization meeting as mayor. In it, you will see the subtle hint that I would, indeed, be a candidate for reelection. After my ill-conceived "political obituary" column and considering the various constituencies I'd alienated—borough employees, teachers, union members, school administrators and school board trustees, among others—it was generally believed that I wouldn't dare run again. A few people picked up on the hints, but I would not make the formal announcement until April, when I declared that I would run as an Independent.

State of the Borough Address—January 1, 2006

Members of the Ramsey Board of Education, other honored guests, colleagues, friends, and fellow citizens of Ramsey—Good afternoon and thank you for attending this 98th annual reorganization meeting of the Ramsey governing body.

Ladies and gentlemen, the state of the Borough is good, but we face challenges that will test the resolve of mayor and council and require nothing less than full cooperation. We must have as our *only* goal the future well being of this community. I'm confident that five out of six council members share that with me. I think the sixth member has that goal in his heart, too, and I will do my best this coming year to gain his support for the important work that lies ahead.

The failure of state government to address financial problems has placed Ramsey and other municipalities at risk. Despite all we've done at our level to control expenses—and we have done a great deal over the past three years—the State of New Jersey lives in a financial house of cards. Governor-elect Corzine says the anticipated deficit for next fiscal year will approach $6 billion, the highest it's been in our state's history. And that's on top of earlier deficits that were closed only by resorting to budget gimmickry, instead of fixing the systemic imbalance that has existed for a decade or more. Thanks to Senator Leonard Lance, one of my favorite state legislators, New Jersey will no longer be able to borrow to meet its operating expenses, as has been the practice of past administrations, both Democratic and Republican. Sen. Lance won a lawsuit in the NJ Supreme Court to block that practice.

In addition to the budget deficit, the state Transportation Trust Fund is about to go broke, unless something is done to shore up its finances. We have known this was coming for years, but so far the state legislature has failed to muster the political courage and non-partisan cooperation to solve the problem. As usual, they wait for problem to develop into crisis before they act. A few weeks ago, the NJ League of Municipalities sent this communication to mayors:

"By June 30, 2006, the Transportation Trust Fund will be completely bankrupt. All $805 million in constitutionally dedicated revenues will be consumed by debt payments. The NJ Department of Transportation and NJ Transit could be forced to shut down. And $150 million in annual Local Aid for municipal and county transportation projects will disappear."

While no one likes the prospect of a hike in the gasoline tax— New Jersey's gas tax is the second lowest in the nation—without that added source of revenue, funds desperately needed for repair of bridges, roads and other infrastructure will not be available. Over the past three years, I have been able to get for Ramsey $685,000 in special grants from the Transportation Trust Fund--$400,000 to replace the DeBaun Avenue Bridge and $285,000 to repair curbs and sidewalks on Wyckoff Avenue. Unless the TTF is fixed, we can no longer anticipate state help in this area.

The state Schools Construction Corp. has turned into a financial nightmare, rife with fraud and abuse. The state committed $6 billion to 31 Abbott districts to construct 346 new school projects. Only 59 were completed before money ran out. The NJ Inspector General found that school construction costs in these districts were 45% higher than construction costs where the state was not involved. The estimate to complete the unfinished projects, which the state is under court order to fund, is $14 billion more. Where will it come from? The state will have to borrow even more money over the next 5 years, and the state budget will suffer further from debt service payments the new borrowing will require.

State pension and benefits programs for government workers are in shambles. Governor Codey's Benefits Review Task Force issued its report last month and bravely set forth an ambitious program to "right" the sinking ship, if our new governor and state legislators have the stomach for it. It will mean going against powerful public employee unions and other special interests. Based on their past performance on controversial issues, I am not optimistic that this problem will be solved any time soon. At least, not until it, too, reaches crisis proportions.

Here are a few quotes from the Task Force report on the subject of health insurance benefits for state and municipal employees.

"The cost of health care, even more than the pension obligation, represents the fastest growing liability to the public employers."

"The Task Force recognizes that health care benefits are inextricably linked to wages and rightly must be negotiated in tandem. However, the Task Force is concerned that while wages are known and increases prescribed, healthcare costs are unknown, not prescribed, and annual increases often far exceed the rate of wage increases."

And, finally, this.

"The Task Force believes that all active and retired employees should share in the cost of health care [benefits]."

In a blistering editorial soon after the Task Force released its report, *The Record* had this to say under the headline, "Finally, a reality check":

"If New Jersey doesn't act to trim public employee benefits and end corruption in the system, the state will have to either substantially increase taxes or slash spending on vital programs. That's how dire the public employee benefits crisis is, according to a timely and incisive report issued last week by a state task force. But the question is can the state and local governments that created the problem now summon the political courage to fix it? Are elected officials willing to even acknowledge the urgency?"

Why have I taken the time to lay out for you in such detail the state's gloomy financial picture? First, it is important that you understand the magnitude of the problem we face in New Jersey. Second, to the extent that the state fails to solve its financial problems, Ramsey and every other municipality will suffer because we will get less state aid. Less aid to municipalities, less aid for our school systems. That means the urgency to put our own financial house in order is greater than ever. We cannot wait for the state to fix anything—not the property tax escalation, not the school funding formula, not the Transportation Trust Fund, not the pension and benefits crisis. We must be the keepers of our own destiny.

Within weeks of taking office three years ago, I saw how the cost of providing free health benefits for our employees was exploding. In 1999, it was $755,000; in 2000, it was $829,000, up 11.8%; in 2001, it was $948,000, up 14.4%; in 2002, it was $1,073,000, up 13.2%; in 2003, it was $1,321,000, up 23.1%.

By 2004, the cost had gone to $1,433,000, up "only" 8.5%. Why the sharp difference in 2004? Because in late 2003, I was able to negotiate with our police union a contract that changed their health benefits to a new program, one that saved the Borough over $100,000 a year. Without that change, the increase in 2004 would have been 17.3%. As it was, the total cost of both health and dental insurance in 2004 was $1,551,000.

I resolved, at the start of my term, not to sign any labor agreement that did not provide for health insurance givebacks. The private sector was requiring its employees to share that expense. What made public sectors employees exempt from that financial reality?

Some argued that public sector employees were paid much less, so therefore they were entitled to free benefits, no matter what the cost to taxpayers. Hogwash. That may have been true ten or twenty years ago, but it is no longer true. A worker today in the Ramsey Water Department earns a monetary package of over $70,000 a year, not counting overtime, after just five years on the job. And they get 30 paid vacation and sick days a year, 13 paid holidays a year, 3 paid personal days a year. They have an excellent pension program, and, oh yes, a wonderful medical and dental insurance benefit. Workers in the Ramsey Water Department earn more money than any water department workers in the surrounding area. They make $10,000 more a year than Allendale, Mahwah, and Ridgewood pay their water department workers.

The cost of a free medical and dental insurance benefit last year was $21,000 for each employee on the family plan. Single benefits cost much less. Since 2003, I've been trying to get employees to share a small part of that cost. How much? About $2,000, with taxpayers picking up the balance. But public sector employees have come to view their benefits as entitlements, and will not willingly give up anything, no matter how reasonable the approach.

Since the police contract, two more unions have agreed to make changes in their benefits, with employees sharing more of the cost of health care. But that was only after we incurred additional legal fees and got a state mediator involved. Three other unions have still not agreed to make any changes. Fortunately, I have had the support of four council members in this long struggle. The other two council members actively worked against me, which is unfortunate. It gave employees false hope that the council would cave in—they haven't and they won't—and it delayed the inevitable, to the employees' detriment and to taxpayers' detriment.

We've already done much, but shall continue to do more to contain all the expenses involved in operating a community our size. Some expenses we have no control over. For example, the state-mandated payment to the employee pension system was zero in 2002. This year, we will have to come up with $400,000 for this line item in our budget.

But let me give you a few examples of the expenses we can control, with a little creativity and good management. This past year, our tax collector retired after many years of distinguished service. We replaced her with a part-time tax collector, who receives no benefits. We had to add another part-time clerk, but the overall savings to the Borough was about $50,000. When a water department worker retired, we didn't replace him. The savings—over $70,000. When a clerical worker filled a vacant deputy court clerk position, we didn't replace her in the clerical position. Rather, we asked for and received greater productivity from the remaining clerical staff. The savings— $40,000. We had three police officers retire last year, and we will not be replacing them until the state financial picture improves drastically. If that means never, then it means never. We can make do with our present police staffing. And that reminds me of another savings. Police overtime in 2002 was $385,000, almost the level as Mahwah, with a department twice our size. The day after I took office, I met with Chief Gurney and Capt. Bailey and told them reducing police overtime would be a priority. I asked for quarterly reports to monitor their progress. Chief Gurney, his superior officers, and the entire department rose to the challenge. In 2005, police overtime was $215,000, down 45% from the 2002 level. The credit goes to Chief Gurney and the entire department. I just pointed them in the right direction.

There is one significant change that I will take sole credit for, because it was I brought the change about. You will recall the borough attorney issue I raised during my run for mayor three years ago. The former borough attorney was costing taxpayers over a quarter of a million a year—more than any other municipality in Bergen County and most of the state was paying for legal services. That issue was a major factor in my landslide victory because it exposed a pitfall of one-party government. The reluctance of party members to publicly challenge their leaders, and absence of checks and balances an opposition party brings to the table.

While you all may be aware of this particular issue, you probably are not aware of the magnitude of the money this one change saved us. So, let me enlighten you. I asked our finance officer to analyze total legal expenses for the three years prior to my taking office— 2000, 2001, and 2002—and to compare that to the total legal expenses for my three years in office—2003, 2004, and 2005. I emphasize that these are the all-inclusive total expense figures, to include labor counsel, attorneys for the planning board and board of adjustment, property tax appeal counsel, and of course, the borough attorney—in other words, the works.

In 2000, our total legal expense was $353,982; in 2001, it was $318,843; in 2002, it was $326,814. The total for the three "pre-Muti" years was $999,639. In 2003, my first year in office after I terminated the former borough attorney, our total legal expense was $144,206; in 2004, it was $166,907; in 2005, even with greatly increased costs for labor counsel because of the union difficulties and other employee matters, the total legal expense was $201,108. The grand total for the three "Muti" years was $508,221. The difference and savings in legal expense: $491,418. Yes, I'm proud of that and I shall continue to take credit for it.

But Ramsey is more than just dollars and cents. With the council's support, we've made major improvements to the quality of life and the way we do business in this community. We became the first town in Bergen County to adopt John's Law II, the law that allows us to keep drunk drivers in jail for up to 8 hours until they sober up, so they don't get back on the road to put themselves and us at risk, like the drunk who killed Ensign John Elliott, the NJ resident the law is named after.

We were the first community in Bergen County to adopt our own anti-"pay-to-play" law and among the first in the state. This ordinance outlaws political contributions by no-bid contractors doing business with the town, and limits such contributions by those intending to do business with us. Sixty more communities have followed the lead of Ramsey, and I intend to propose to the council this year an even tougher ordinance dealing with this subject.

If you've attended a Ramsey Wind Symphony concert in the last three years, you've felt the pride in having our own community band, just as we did a century ago. Not only for the patriotic concerts these fine musicians, led by maestro Peter Del Vecchio, perform on July 4th weekend and Ramsey Day, but also for the young people's concert each March, classical concert in November, and jazz and show tunes concerts in summer. All free. The annual property tax impact for this year-round beautiful music? About $1.40 per family.

We resurrected and funded the Ramsey Fine Arts Council, which brings you the wonderful summer concert series, the Ramsey Day art show, and the fall harvest festival, among other activities. The annual tax impact per family? About $2.80. And we've started the planning for our Centennial in two years. It will be the grandest celebration you've ever seen.

I could go on and on, but I think you get the picture. This is not an easy task—governing a community like Ramsey. We don't always get everything right, but we always *try* to get everything right. You've got some very good people on this governing body working for you. I don't know who will occupy this chair next year, but there are certainly people in this room right now who would be viable candidates, based on their experience and accomplishments.

I don't like the idea of uncontested races for any public office, as was the situation in Ramsey before I ran in November of 2002. The mettle of a mayoral candidate or council candidate should be tested in the public forum of ideas. His or her record and accomplishments should be examined. The hard questions should be put to the candidates, and their answers scrutinized. These positions are too important to be handed to someone without opposition.

So, whoever the Republican candidate for mayor is, I hope there will be an opponent. So far, I have not heard any names mentioned, but I expect someone with the grit, the determination, the creativity, the experience, and the ability to do a good job will eventually come forward. Who knows, it might even be someone you're already familiar with.

Chapter 37

In April 2006, I declared my intention to run for reelection by placing this open letter to Ramsey residents in the local newspaper.

A Candidate with a Difference

Dear Friends and Fellow Citizens of Ramsey:

Yes, I am a candidate for reelection, but with a difference. In November, I shall run as an Independent.

Partisanship has no place in local government. There is no Republican way or Democratic way to provide municipal services, but only the innovative, business-like way all elected officials should follow, regardless of party affiliation. Becoming an Independent is a natural extension of that belief.

Although I've carried out my duties as mayor without regard for party politics, getting council Republicans to support my reform agenda wasn't easy. After controlling Ramsey for 16 years, the last eight without opposition in any election, they weren't happy about my challenging the status quo.

How did I gain their cooperation? For one thing, I'm not easily intimidated; their 4-2 majority didn't stop me from proposing ideas to make Ramsey government more efficient and responsive. I studied the problems we faced and was unafraid to tackle difficult issues. As any former Navy pilot will tell you, after you've landed a plane on the pitching deck of a carrier, no task is too daunting.

My firm stance in union negotiations to bring health insurance costs under control is one example. That approach is bearing fruit, although, understandably, it has made me unpopular among borough employees. I deeply regret that. Ramsey's employees are hard-working, decent people with families to support. I respect every one of them. But you didn't elect me to win popularity contests.

Something had to be done to curtail this expense, which was rising by 15-20% a year. Clearly, employees would have to contribute more toward the cost of their benefits, a bitter pill for anyone to swallow. I acted in the most humane and reasonable way I could by offering salary "bump-ups" so they weren't totally out-of-pocket because of increased co-pays. We could afford to do that because insurance premium savings were greater than the salary bump-ups.

One by one, unions began accepting the new insurance plan. It was still an excellent benefits package for employees, and, with the savings it generated, the Borough's financial outlook improved. After one union settled following two years of negotiations, the shop steward came into my office, shut the door, and said, "You know, Mayor, you were being fair with us from the start. We had blinders on and just couldn't see it." I appreciated her candor. Needless to say, the image of a fair and reasonable Mayor Muti never made it to the newspapers.

The Republicans are gearing up for an all-out fight to regain full control of Ramsey's government. Apparently, holding six out of six council seats is not enough. They don't want a possible opposing voice at the table. That may be bad for them, but I think you'll agree one-party domination of Ramsey government, no matter which party, is a disaster for taxpayers. Things may have been more tranquil before I became mayor, but we were headed toward a financial "perfect storm" because no one had the fortitude to challenge wasteful expenditures or address difficult issues.

Because I've been outspoken on important but controversial matters—while others remained comfortably silent—I'm an underdog in this election. But I shall put my trust in the people of Ramsey. If there were issues on which we disagreed or areas where I fell short, I hope you'll conclude the successes outweigh the failures. Please know that the single guiding principle behind every stand I've taken is the best interests of Ramsey—the town where I was born and raised, the town that I love.

Sincerely,

Richard Muti

Chapter 38

Another Op-Ed piece in The Record, published on February 3, 2005. It uses my favored reference to Pogo, the political comic strip character of the 1940s and -50s.

The "Pogo Factor" in Local Government

Confronted with a $4-5 billion budget deficit for fiscal 2006, Governor Codey says everything will be "on the table" to close the gap. I applaud the governor's candor; clearly, he has no choice. But that does not bode well for local government. Costs previously taken for granted, like free health insurance benefits for public employees, are mushrooming. Established communities with little remaining land for development can no longer rely on an expanding tax base for revenue. Double-digit tax rate increases, I predict, will be the norm this municipal budget season. How, then, are municipalities to deal with shrinking state aid, rising local costs, and stagnant tax bases? How do we survive what promises to be an economic "perfect storm"?

The old "Pogo" comic strip provides insight. Old-timers like me can picture Pogo, the intrepid opossum, wearing a paper admiral's hat and standing, wooden sword raised high, in the prow of a leaky rowboat. Taking a turn on Oliver Hazard Perry's famous naval quote, Pogo declares to the world: "We have met the enemy, and he is us!" Sadly, when it comes to local government finances, we elected officials are, too often, our own worst enemy

Sure, we can blame Trenton for our problems—there is certainly justification. State legislators will always embrace the political shell game of enacting laws to *cure* society's ills, real or imagined, without worrying about where the money will come from to implement those laws. The money will come from property tax payers.

Nevertheless, there is much local government leaders can do for themselves, if they have the stamina and political courage to make a stand in at least one key area: labor contracts. If your community is like mine, salaries and benefits make up two-thirds of the municipal budget. Yet, those costs are probably the most controllable part of municipal expenses.

Benefits—health insurance benefits, in particular—are eating us alive. In Ramsey, the cost of providing free health insurance to municipal employees increased by 23% in 2003, with double digit increases in the two prior years. The 2004 cost to the Borough of a free family-plan insurance policy was $17,206 per employee, up 17%. In total, this budget line item was $1.5 million in 2004; left unchecked, it will become $3.7 million four years from now, if insurance rates continue rising at that pace.

It should be clear to any reasonable person that something must be done, but try explaining that to the union shop steward in your town. It has been my experience, after seven years of negotiating public employee contracts on behalf of government employers, that the union response to employer attempts at cost containment is this: "That's your problem; we want what's coming to us." Most public employee unions will not make the slightest concession voluntarily, even when the concession does its members no harm.

All five of Ramsey's employee union contracts expired the day I took office two years ago. Municipal workers had supported my ticket, but when I began to assert myself in labor negotiations within weeks of taking office, the honeymoon was over. I was willing to soften the blow for current employees by adjusting salary levels to help offset their added insurance cost. But I also wanted more substantial changes for future employees, including shared premiums.

One would think that such an approach would work, but results have been mixed. Usually, public employee unions do not hesitate to give up "the unborn." They will make concessions regarding future employees, so long as current employees remain well fed. That may help municipalities ten or fifteen years down the road;

but in the public sector, where turnover is minimal, it does little to alleviate short-term financial concerns. Clearly, a dual approach is needed: incremental changes now, big changes later.

The time is ripe for confronting public sector employees about their "entitlements." Labor arbitrators will have to acknowledge skyrocketing insurance costs and tightening revenue. They will have no choice but to grant reasonable employer proposals to bring costs under control, especially when municipalities press the matter in court by appealing unfair decisions. We can reach fair settlements in municipal labor negotiations—fair to valued employees and fair to beleaguered property tax payers—but the effort will require strong government leaders, able to withstand union pressure and willing to put aside partisan gamesmanship.

Chapter 39

This was my 54th and last "In the Arena" column as mayor.   It follows a familiar theme of pride in my heritage.

"Give me your tired, your poor . . ."

". . . your huddled masses yearning to breathe free, the wretched refuse of your teeming shore, send these, the homeless, tempest-tost to me, I lift my lamp beside the golden door." We all remember this excerpt from Emma Lazarus's famous poem, "The New Colossus," written in 1883 to raise money for the Statue of Liberty.   I relate to the image conveyed by the poem.   My four grandparents fit the profile: dirt-poor immigrants from southern Italy, who left behind family, friends, and the "old country" to find a new life in America.

Now, everyone can trace his or her immigrant roots, thanks to a website that allows access to Ellis Island records: www.ellisisland. org. You'll need the correct name of your forebear who entered this country. I found the actual ships' manifests for all four grandparents, giving their dates of arrival in this country, their places of residence and ports of departure in Italy, and other remarkably detailed information.

My paternal grandmother, Rosaria Potenza, was just 17 when she made the crossing in 1907.   She did it on her own, with a younger sister in tow.   I still remember her story of the "tempest-tost" sea voyage they endured in steerage, Grandma's first and last encounter with a boat.   In later life, an immersed ankle was the most she would venture at Coney Island or the Jersey shore, so great was her dread of the ocean.   But she was fearless in every other aspect of her life. Her husband died in 1929, and she raised nine children in Ramsey on her own during the height of the Great Depression. What a remarkable, giant of a woman, all 4 feet, 11 inches of her. She died in 1970 on one of the saddest days of my life.

Sergio Muti, born in Molfetta on the Adriatic coast, was 23 and single when he arrived on November 8, 1906; he would later meet and be smitten by Rosaria. He could neither read nor write Italian, nor could he speak English well. He didn't have a cent in his pocket. One of the categories on the ship's manifest was whether an immigrant had $50 in his or her possession. If not, the immigration official was to write down the lesser amount possessed. In my grandfather's case, this official had written down $10, but then crossed it out and put in a "0". Sergio was 5 feet, 2 inches, dark complexioned, with no scars or identifying marks. His final destination was Hoboken, NJ, where he was to stay with his older brother. My grandfather moved to Ramsey in 1911.

On my mother's side, Giuseppe Milano, 20 years old, arrived on May 13, 1910. He was born in a village north of Rome. His actual name was *Milana*, but the person who wrote the manifest made the final "a" look like an "o". Grandpa and his family have been known as *Milano* ever since. At 5 feet, 4 inches, my maternal grandfather was the tallest of my grandparents. He was also the richest, having $50 in his pocket at his arrival. Grandpa Joe lived to be 95.

Pia Remia, my maternal grandmother, was the last to get here, on August 26, 1913. She, too, was just 17 and met my grandfather after they both were in this country. Giuseppe and Pia settled in Waldwick in 1915, along with many of Grandpa's *paisani* from the same village in Italy. Most of them worked as laborers for the railroad.

I think you get the picture. I am very proud of my grandparents and my Italian heritage, something I share with more than 25% of Ramsey residents. We are the largest ethnic group in town, followed by those with Irish heritage and those with German heritage. Sergio, Rosaria, Giuseppe, and Pia—all of them just kids, really—crossed an ocean with hardly a nickel to their names, no education, and very little in the way of prospects. Nothing except a willingness to work long hours for very low pay. In my mind, they were as brave and adventurous as the pioneers who crossed America's great expanse in the 1800s to settle the West.

Chapter 40

This was the last time I addressed Ramsey residents as mayor. The speech was delivered on December 13, 2006, to one of the largest crowds to attend a regular meeting of the mayor and council—about 80 people showed up to hear my swan song, some, no doubt, to make sure I was really leaving.

The Mayor's "Last Meeting" Address

It has been a good four years. Good for me personally and, I hope, good for the Borough of Ramsey. For my part, I get to end my 32 years of public service—first as a naval officer, then as a career prosecutor, and finally as mayor—in a job that knew no bounds of personal fulfillment. Just think . . . to be mayor of one's hometown— the place that nurtured me, that educated me, that sent me out into the world ready to strive and prepared to achieve. Yes, there were personal trials and a few setbacks during my tenure, but they were far outweighed by the satisfaction of having helped hundreds of residents with their individual problems and the expressions of gratitude they gave me in return, often with the comment that no other public official had ever taken an interest.

I took an interest, not only in the immediate needs of residents, but also in the broader needs of the community as a whole. Sometimes that broader perspective conflicted with the interests of individuals or smaller groups. When that happens, a leader tries to minimize the adverse impact on the individual, but is duty-bound to put the interests of the community first, long-term interests as well as short-term interests, no matter what the political cost.

Nowhere was this conflict of interests more apparent than with the employee health benefits issue.

Collectively speaking, we in Ramsey are fortunate in having an outstanding group of employees—certainly the finest I've ever encountered in my years of public service. Almost without exception, they go out of their way to assist residents, even though manpower in several departments has been reduced. We have fewer employees in administration, fewer in tax collection, fewer in the road department, and fewer in the water department than when I entered office. This was by design. One way to reduce expenses is to *not* automatically replace retiring employees, but to look for ways to maintain services with fewer people—like sharing a tax collector with a neighboring community to save $65,000 a year in salary and benefits, as we did when our long-time tax collector retired.

And how did the mayor respond to this wonderfully productive group of employees? By cutting their benefits. Coldhearted, some said. Ungrateful. Insensitive. I can think of dozens of pejoratives.

The hard, inescapable truth is that I had no choice but to make the difficult decision to cut back on employee benefits. Health insurance costs had been going up 15-23% for years. Left unchecked, these benefit costs would have consumed a fifth of the Borough's operating budget in just five years. We owed it to Ramsey taxpayers to do something.

This should have been attended to years earlier, but there was no political will to do so. It fell to me, then, with the support of a council majority, to implement the changes that were necessary for Ramsey's financial future.

Progress has been gradual, but deliberate. First the police union agreed to a new contract and accepted a reduction in health benefits that saves the Borough $100,000 a year. That's $100,000 a year, each and every year in the future, starting in 2004. Then the water department union agreed to a small reduction; then the clerical and library unions agreed to much larger reductions. Then the water department union, in a subsequent contract, accepted even greater changes—breakthrough provisions that, for the first time, required regular employee contributions toward their insurance premium costs and granted other significant concessions.

More remains to be done, but let me tell you the full dollar impact of what we have achieved to date. In 2003, the year I took office, but before I was able to put changes into place through union negotiations, health insurance costs increased by 23% over 2002 and had been going up at double-digits rates for five years. In 2004, the increase dropped to 19%; then, in 2005, as changes began to kick in, it dropped to 15% and we got a sizeable refund on our premium, about $120,000. In 2006, just this year, the increase dropped to 5%, the lowest in at least the last ten years—I haven't researched farther back than that.

Our insurance carrier—Horizon Blue Cross/Blue Shield—attributed this amazing result to the lower claims they had to pay, largely because of the changes we made to employee benefits. Because our insurance plan is rated prospectively, we get a refund when claims are down. But that isn't the end of the good news.

Earlier this month, I received a letter from Horizon—we will be getting a refund of $300,000 on the 2006 premium to apply toward next year's premium. That represents a 20% drop in the cost and is the largest refund in Ramsey's history according to Borough Administrator Nick Saros. Furthermore, it comes at a time when costs are rising all over the industry. For the first time ever, our net health insurance premium cost in the upcoming year will be less than the year before, and not just by a little. Our net cost will be 15% less in 2007 than it was in 2006. I haven't done the research, but I would be willing to wager that no other town in New Jersey has experienced this turnaround in the last four years. It did not happen by accident, ladies and gentlemen.

After all the ballots were counted in the election last month, the final vote difference between Chris Botta and myself was 189 votes. A number of my supporters have asked if I regret running as an Independent, instead of on the Democratic line. The Democratic candidate—who never spoke out on any issue, who attended just three or four council meetings the entire year before the election, and who ran a campaign that was remarkable only for its lack of substance—nevertheless managed to poll more than 800 votes. Surely, my friends asked, most of those votes would have gone to you, mayor.

Perhaps, but running in the Bergen County Democratic Organization column was never an option for me. I did run on their line the first time, but since then I've learned things about the way this political machine runs Bergen County that repulse me.

Unfortunately, I think this organization will continue to control county government for the next decade or more. They generate significant campaign contributions through their pay-to-play methods and continue to outspend Republicans by ten or twenty to one. Bergen County Democrats remain a powerful machine, well-oiled by money. Bergen County Republicans are disorganized, fractious and pathetic in their attempts to meet this challenge. The status quo will remain the same, I am afraid. Apparently, voters attach little importance to ethics in politics. As long as the public succumbs to slick, negative advertising and superficial claims, without taking the time to understand the issues, it will get the type of government it deserves.

I have written articles for *The Record* and have spoken out against the Bergen County Democratic Organization. It was that group who put up the Democratic candidate for mayor, simply for the purpose of siphoning off votes that may have gone to me. I was their target—they had no interest in serving the residents of Ramsey. Their scheme worked, just as they planned. I have never questioned their political astuteness, only their moral values.

Councilman Botta was the beneficiary of this political intrigue. But he is a good man and deserves a chance on his own merits to lead this community. But keep one thing in mind. The most interesting number in the election was not the 189 votes that separated him and me, but rather the almost 4,000 eligible voters who did not bother to vote for the office of mayor.

Mr. Botta served the community well as a councilman for six years. I served well, I think, as mayor for four years. Both of us did so at great personal sacrifice. None of that mattered to 40% of the electorate, who simply chose to stay home on November 7th. In my case, 75% of registered voters either didn't care who would be their mayor or preferred someone else. Mr. Botta's percentage was slightly better—73% didn't care or preferred someone else.

The logical question that arises from those stark facts is this: Was it worth it? Spending all that time on the public's business— meeting after meeting, night after night—when a majority of the public didn't seem to notice or care?

I think I can answer for both of us. We don't serve for personal accolades, for personal ambition or gain. We serve the public out of love for this community; we serve because of a fervent desire to make things better. Our reward is the satisfaction of knowing we made a difference. For both of us, I think, that is reward enough.

Chapter 41

The year before I became mayor, I founded an organization I called the Ramsey Civic Association. Fifty or sixty public-minded residents joined me to encourage more substantive political discourse in our town. When I became a candidate for mayor, I stepped down as chairman of the group, but left a very able leader in charge. The RCA is still going today. I drew up this list of demands, hoping we could get a movement going throughout the state. Unfortunately, it didn't take hold. But I still like what I wrote. It reads like a plain language, good government manifesto, exactly what I intended it to be.

WE, THE PEOPLE, *DEMAND*

We, the undersigned citizens of Ramsey and other New Jersey towns, make the following demands on our elected leaders and all candidates for elective office:

We, the people, *demand* that you treat us like intelligent human beings and communicate with us using "straight talk," not media sound bites and not half-truths. We are fed up with "spin doctors," no matter what their political party.

We, the people, *demand* that you bring ethics back to state and local government. We're tired of being the laughingstock of the nation when it comes to political corruption. Put crooked public officials in prison and take away their pensions. Appoint judges who respect the public trust and who will come down hard on those who violate it. Stop giving no-bid government contracts to big campaign donors; it may not be illegal, but it stinks and we don't like it.

We, the people, *demand* that you start treating us as the special interest most worthy of your attention. We don't care what powerful political forces in this state have given you campaign contributions or other promises of support. You are beholden to us, not to the special interests.

We, the people, *demand* that you put partisan bickering aside and work together. We are tired of the blame game. New Jersey is facing enormous problems because both Republicans and Democrats have let us down. Enough! Get us out of the mess you created. We, the people, *demand* action, not political rhetoric, in the following areas:

1. Relying on property taxes as the primary source of public education funding is unfair. It is driving seniors from our communities, forcing them to relocate away from family, friends, doctors, and other health service providers. We want the property tax problem fixed . . . now! Thirty school districts—the so-called "Abbott" districts—should not be receiving half of all state aid to public education. Distribute state aid more equitably. If it is going to take a constitutional amendment to accomplish that, then do it.

2. Stop borrowing money to pay for operating expenses and coming up with gimmicks to balance the budget. We're tired of seeing huge deficits every year. We want you to spend our money more wisely and eliminate waste. If you need more revenue to put us on a sound financial footing, have the political courage to say so. But cut spending as much as you can FIRST, before you come running to us for more money.

3. Fix the Transportation Trust Fund. We don't want to see our roads, bridges and other infrastructure deteriorate further. And we don't want to lose federal funds for some of these projects because we can't provide matching funds. You have a habit of putting off difficult decisions until they reach crisis proportions. We don't like that kind of planning.

4. Public employees are going to have to realize that times have changed. We can no longer afford to give them the gold-plated benefits packages they have enjoyed in the past. They must lower their expectations and accept labor contracts more in line with the private sector. Do something about the huge projected

deficit in the pension system. You've got to stop enacting union-backed laws that hinder local government and school districts in their attempts to bring public salaries and benefits under control. You are going to have to find the courage somewhere to stand up to public employee unions. Put the public interest first, not your reelection prospects.

Chapter 42

A letter-to-the-editor, my last written communication to Ramsey residents before leaving office. Unfortunately, it calls them to task, gently, for being AWOL on a special day.

Veterans' Day—2006

I read somewhere we are losing WWII vets at a rate of 1,000 a day, a rate that will soar in coming years. Twenty years from now, we'll be down to a handful of these men and women of the "Greatest Generation"—a precious and irreplaceable handful.

In Ramsey, at this year's Veterans' Day ceremonies, the VFW was missing two of its stalwarts—my friend Tony Galasso and Jim Alcaro—both of whom passed away this year. Tony's wife Connie was there to represent her beloved husband, as was Jim Alcaro's family, most notably young Mary Alcaro, Jim's granddaughter.

A few years back, Mary, then an eighth grader, wrote a beautiful letter-to-the editor in praise of our nation's veterans. Lee Fisher, deputy VFW post commander, remembered and asked Mary to read her letter at this year's ceremonies. What a stirring moment it was to hear this young woman, as her proud mother and father looked on, acknowledge what we all owe to our veterans.

Ramsey Police Chief Bryan Gurney spoke eloquently of his family's involvement in our nation's wars, including his brave young son now serving in the thick of action in Iraq and his son's best friend, struck down by a sniper's bullet just a few weeks ago. Thank you, Chief Gurney, and God bless your son and keep him from harm.

Dear friends and fellow citizens of Ramsey, I must tell you I was disheartened by the poor attendance at this year's ceremonies. It was a beautiful, warm fall day, and as a Ramsey High School student played Taps at the end of the 20-minute program, I couldn't help but reflect on the fact that, of Ramsey's almost 15,000 residents, less than 20 could find the time to attend. I know we all honor these wonderful men and women who fought so bravely in by-gone wars and who are fighting and dying now, even as you read this letter, in a raging war with no end in sight. Please, in future, let us all demonstrate—for them and their families, before these old timers are gone—the honor and respect we all feel in our hearts. Let us stand with them on their special days of remembrance, as they stood up for us when our democracy was in peril.

Chapter 43

This Op-Ed article (The Record, June 21, 2007) responded to the state legislature's proposed law banning dual office-holding. Not surprisingly, they took the easy way out, failing to address the real problems associated with that practice.

In Defense of "Double-Dippers"

In the rush to outlaw dual office holding in New Jersey, no one is addressing what we stand to lose by banning local elected officials from also serving in the state legislature. The law of unintended consequences may one day give us reason to regret this action.

Mayors and council members are in the trenches every day in the war against rising property taxes, striving to overcome obstacles like unfunded mandates, arbitration rules that favor public employee unions over municipalities, and bureaucratic make-work measures with no discernable public benefit. Obstacles thrown in their way by out-of-touch state legislators, more intent on following an easy path to reelection than on finding solutions to the problems besetting us. Remove these local "double-dippers" from the state legislature and you remove the last vestige of elected officials who really know the hardships faced at the local level—the people who must balance annual budgets without gimmicks and quick fixes, or face the ire of friends and neighbors down at town hall if they fail to measure up. Remove them, and you take away the champions of the little guy, John Q. Taxpayer.

Except for a few large cities, local office holders in New Jersey are part-timers. Unless retired or independently wealthy, these elected officials must have other employment to support their families. If they receive any compensation at all for their municipal service, most likely it isn't even enough to pay their own property taxes. State legislators are also part-timers, and most of them, I expect, also hold outside jobs to earn a living. There is no conflict, therefore, in having two part-time positions that are compatible with each other in terms of time requirements.

The reason most often cited against dual office holding is the alleged conflict of interest when these legislators sponsor legislation or take policy positions solely benefiting their own municipalities. *The Record* contends that such "elected officials cannot ably serve two masters." It is a red herring issue. First of all, it takes a majority to pass legislation and a governor to sign it, not one mayor looking to cadge an extra hundred thousand for his hometown. Second, for a "double-dipper" to get such narrow legislation passed would require unbelievable collusion among other legislators, four-fifths of whom do not hold local elective office. I suppose it may be argued that groups of legislators will follow the "you scratch my back and I'll scratch yours" rule of pork barrel legislation, but dual office holding is not the genesis of that pernicious practice, nor is a ban on dual office holding the cure.

And what of other potential conflicts? What about the lawyer legislator who votes for legislation having a beneficial effect on the legal profession? Or, the union leader legislator who promotes policies that favor union members? Or, the engineer legislator who sponsors a bill that has a side effect of helping the construction industry? There is a difference between a true conflict of interest, which requires the honest public official to refrain from acting in the matter, and an imagined conflict of interest, one not likely to arise in the real world. If legislators cannot tell the difference, they should be prosecuted or voted out of office.

The legislature, at Governor Corzine's urging, will likely pass a bill this month to ban dual office holding. It will be the Democratic version that prevails, since that party controls both houses and the governorship. It outlaws the practice after February 2008, a convenience for the 19 current dual officer holders now serving in the legislature. They will be allowed to keep both their state legislative posts and their local elected positions for as long as they want to, having been "grandfathered in." The legislation does nothing to get rid of more serious affronts to sound public policy, like the powerful state legislator who gets a no-show job at a public university, thereby enhancing his public pension two- or three-fold, and then generates special grants for that university; or, the state legislator who takes a "consulting" job with a hospital, and then steers public money in the direction of his employer; or, the "fat cat" county political boss who controls a half dozen or more state legislators and uses that power to further his own interests; or, the lawyer as state legislator who uses his influence to string together multiple *paid but not elected* public jobs.

The soon-to-be-enacted ban on dual office holding is a distraction, designed to show our state legislators acting the part of decisive lawmakers. In reality, they are attacking the least offensive aspect of dual office holding—one that may very well be beneficial to the public at large—and ignoring harder aspects of the problem that may threaten their own interests.

So what else is new?

Chapter 44

The Mayor's Report Card

At the start of my four years at the helm of my hometown, I spoke of how I wished to be judged.

> "*Acta, non verba.* Actions, not words. From this moment forward, measure me by my actions and the actions of my administration, not by my words."
>
> Mayor Richard Muti
> Ramsey Reorganization Meeting
> January 5, 2003

Here, then, is a self-evaluation—not overly modest in relating the pluses, but also not reticent in acknowledging the minuses.

First, the pluses:

1. With a council majority aligned against me, I managed to rid Ramsey of a borough attorney who had been gouging taxpayers for years, with the acquiescence of the former mayor and six councilmen. This one act saved $500,000 during my four years in office and will continue to save at least $100,000 a year going forward—all without diminution in either the quality or quantity of legal representation.

2. Within weeks of taking office, I saw the upward spiral of employee health insurance costs and devised a plan to deal with it—a two-pronged approach that sought modest, incremental changes with existing employees, asking them to absorb some of the cost, and

more significant changes with future employees, who would have the free choice of working for Ramsey or not. I personally took charge of contract negotiations with six unions and announced that I would not sign a union contract that did not have health insurance give-backs. Four unions made concessions before I left office; two unions dug in their heels and refused to make concessions, so, when I left office, they did not have a contract and were earning 2002 wages. As a result of the changes made, the annual increase in health insurance premiums went from 23% in 2003 to 5% in 2006, plus we got a $300,000 refund on our 2005 premium to offset costs in 2007.

3. During my campaign in 2002, I raised concerns about a bank's plan to install a helistop at its Ramsey branch, in the middle of a commercial and residential area. The application had been moving through the approval process, and no one was raising the safety issue or taking steps to insure it would be addressed. With help from key residents and supporters, we questioned the mayor and council and planning board and brought the matter to the public's attention. People packed the meeting rooms to demand action. The day after my election, I announced I would conduct a hearing into the safety issues. The bank withdrew its application the next day.

4. Using the NJ Common Cause model as a guide, I wrote Ramsey's ordinance outlawing pay-to-play, the pernicious practice that allows attorneys, engineers, and other no-bid contractors to make political contributions to the elected officials who would then decide on their appointments and remuneration. I proposed it to the council and won their support. Ramsey became the first municipality in Bergen County to enact an anti-pay-to-play ordinance and one of the first in the state. A year or two later, the state and county followed suit, but with weaker versions of the law. A year before leaving office, I tried to get the council to enact a tougher local ordinance, but they tabled the matter until I had left office. Soon after my departure, the new administration enacted my proposed tougher law.

5. I proposed that Ramsey adopt "John's Law II," named after Navy Ensign John Elliott, who was tragically killed by a drunk driver while traveling home to New Jersey from the Naval Academy

for his mother's birthday. The council followed my lead and Ramsey became the first town in Bergen County to put John's Law II on its books. This law allows the police department to keep drunk drivers behind bars until their blood alcohol levels reach a safe level.

6. Ramsey has its own community band again, after 60 or 70 years without one, because of an idea I had after the "Ramapo" Wind Symphony played at the 2003 Reorganization Meeting. With council support, we agreed to give a modest budget allocation to the band for music and other expenses ($10,000), and the band became the Ramsey Wind Symphony. It changed its home base to our town and provided free concerts attended by tens of thousands of residents during my tenure as mayor.

7. I re-started the tradition of having a Fourth of July Weekend concert and fireworks display in Ramsey. In the early days of our town's history, this was an annual occurrence, along with a parade. But the tradition of celebrating our nation's birthday fell by the wayside decades ago. It wasn't even done when I was growing up in Ramsey. This new annual event began in 2003 and took place each year thereafter. The Ramsey Wind Symphony provides an outstanding patriotic concert, capped off by fireworks, to each year's audience of about 5,000 people.

8. The average increase in the municipal tax rate (the portion attributable to municipal government and not to the schools or county) during my four years as mayor was below the rate of inflation. It took a cooperative effort between myself and a majority of the council to achieve this result, which was unequaled by any town in our area.

9. Within months of taking office, I proposed and got approval from the council for a clothing allowance stipend for members of the Ramsey Ambulance Corps. The fire department and rescue squad had been receiving the stipend for years—it was a great aid in their recruitment of new members and retention of old members. But ambulance corps members had been denied that benefit, and their recruitment and retention were suffering. There was talk of having to go to a paid ambulance service during daytime hours. With the institution of this new

benefit, recruitment and retention soared, and I left office with the Ramsey Ambulance Corps having the healthiest membership status in many years.

10. I proposed and the Council enacted a tax on motel and hotel rooms in the Borough of Ramsey. This tax is collected from transients staying over in our town for one reason or another, people who are not residents and who pay no real estate taxes to support services they might have occasion to use, like police, fire, ambulance, road maintenance, and the like. Two councilmen voted against the measure. During my four years as mayor, it brought in over $400,000 in extra revenue to help support Borough operations—revenue that did not have to be collected from our residents in real estate taxes.

11. While in office, I personally obtained, through my own initiative and not as part of any routine applications, $760,000 in state grants. This money was used to pay for projects like the Wyckoff Avenue curbs and sidewalks and the DeBaun Avenue bridge. Once again, we didn't have to resort to real estate tax money to complete these necessary projects.

12. I proposed, wrote, and guided through enactment a law to prevent "adult businesses" from opening in Ramsey within one mile of a school, church, playground, or park. Previously, there was no zoning prohibition against such establishments opening anywhere in our town.

13. I proposed, wrote, and guided through enactment a law establishing rules and procedures for the filming and taping of public meetings. The genesis of this law was the desire to prevent children attending public meetings—as scouts, athletes, and other students often do—from being filmed and their identities shown on the Internet without parents' permission. Afterwards, a state appellate court later upheld the right of municipalities to do exactly what our law allows us to do—set reasonable guidelines.

14. I vetoed a measure by the council to increase the pay of the mayor and council members. It was the only veto I cast as mayor. The council backed down and upheld my veto. They have not tried to raise their pay since then.

15. I proposed that the 2003 budget allocate $20,000 for the resurrection and support of the Ramsey Fine Arts Council, which had disbanded during the tenure of the prior administration because of a lack of leadership and funding. The council agreed to it. In subsequent years, I obtained corporate contributions that raised the funding level without using more taxpayer dollars. The RFAC provided a wonderful summer concert series, a fall harvest festival attended by a thousand or more adults and children each year, and other opportunities for families to enjoy the arts.

16. Visit the council chambers and you will see beautifully framed portraits of all our mayors throughout our 100 year history. It was I who rescued these portraits from storage and had them put on permanent display. The council had considered them old-fashioned and out of place in the newly remodeled Borough Hall. I considered them part of Ramsey's heritage. While mayor, I conducted tours of the Borough Hall for cub scouts and brownie troops. These kids loved hearing about our history and community leaders.

17. I started the practice of giving out "Mayor's Awards" at each reorganization meeting to outstanding volunteers and citizen activists in our community. It was done at my own expense, and by the time I left office, I had made almost thirty such awards. The new mayor has continued the practice.

18. I never missed a meeting of the governing body while mayor. Vacations, personal business, family responsibilities—everything took second place to conducting the public's business at our official meetings.

19. While serving on the Board of Public Works as mayor and chairman, I saved Borough residents more than $1 million in capital expenditures, as documented in the minutes.

20. I served on the NJ League of Municipalities Legislative Committee for four years, traveling to Trenton each month to review and discuss proposed legislation affecting the well being of New Jersey's 566 municipalities.

21. I regained control of the large municipal parking lot across from the Borough Hall. For years, it had been assumed that the State owned this property; I disputed that belief, did the research,

and got the valuable resource back under the auspices of the Borough of Ramsey.

22. I negotiated a contract with United Water that gave Ramsey more than $250,000 in extra benefits—improvements made to our infrastructure at their expense and not taxpayers' expense. In addition, UW repaved every street they disturbed, curb to curb, and the library parking lot.

23. I formed the Centennial Committee in 2003 to start the planning process for Ramsey's 100th birthday celebration in 2008 and put the former mayor, my political opponent, in charge of it.

24. New Jersey mayors are permitted by law to collect fees for performing marriage ceremonies. I donated all such fees to Ramsey organizations like the boy scouts, girl scouts, senior citizens, Ramsey baseball, soccer and football associations, the Ramsey Free Public Library, and the Ramsey Band and Color Guard Parents' Association. Over my four years, more than $5,000 reached these fine organizations from this initiative.

25. I started what I hope will become a tradition—naming a long-standing citizen of Ramsey, with a strong record of participation in community affairs, as the Grand Marshal of the Ramsey Day Parade. It was a way to honor these pillars of our community at no cost to taxpayers.

26. I negotiated a cap on engineering fees that our consultant to the Board of Public Works could charge, resulting in more than $100,000 in annual savings.

27. I raised more than $40,000 in private contributions to the Centennial Committee and Fine Arts Council.

28. I negotiated a police union contract—the first voluntary contract, without binding arbitration, in 10 years—that resulted in the lowest pay increase in any northern New Jersey police department for the 4-year duration of the contract. The police received something they wanted and deserved—a retirement health insurance package similar to what other departments received and one that saved them money and the Borough money, too, by encouraging earlier retirements. In addition, they converted

to a less expensive health insurance plan, resulting in another $100,000 annual savings for taxpayers.

29. I was the first mayor of Ramsey to be a graduate of the Ramsey Public School system, K-12.

30. My father and I are the first father-son pair to serve on the governing body of Ramsey. My father was councilman for nine years, five as president, and I served as mayor for four years.

And now, the minuses:

1. I could have handled labor negotiations with our employees better. No, I don't mean that I should have given them more—I couldn't do that without risking Ramsey's financial future. But I should have listened more and talked less. I don't know that I could have achieved any better results, but with a different approach—not weaker, but more empathetic—employees may not have felt so alienated.

2. I think I tried to do too much, too soon. In my inaugural address on January 5, 2003, I said that I would approach change gradually, seeking consensus and striving to work closely with my council colleagues. In the political atmosphere of the first two years, I think I was too intent on pushing *my* reform agenda forward. Perhaps there was a way I could have allowed the council to be a greater part of that process.

3. I've already mentioned my misguided run for the state senate in 2003. It cost me dearly in citizen support, personal finances, and stress. And it caused a distraction from what I hoped to accomplish in Ramsey, my number one priority.

4. I don't apologize for my opposition to selling beer on Ramsey Day, but my raising, at that same time, the issue of consolidating the fire department and rescue squad was wrong. Most rescue squads in New Jersey are part of the local fire department. Ramsey's arrangement of separate organizations is unusual. But it is the structure we have, and a merger of the two units would have caused morale problems. In response to the mayor's meddling, the rescue squad reinvented itself, and became an even more valuable asset to the community. Nevertheless, there will come a time when we must guard against too great

a duplication of expensive capital equipment, for both fire and rescue. For example, we have a fire/rescue vehicle in the fire department that could easily have served as a second rescue truck. Instead, the prior administration bought a second rescue truck. We need to come up with a better plan for emergency services, one that takes into consideration the assets of nearby towns and cooperative agreements with those towns.

5. It took four years to get the downtown beautification program done. I should have pushed harder to get it completed sooner. There were other engineering projects that took too long to get done. We had a very good borough engineer, but I think we overloaded him with projects. We should have come up with a more efficient plan to accomplish that function. There were far too many delays in the Construction Department, too—again, not because those employees didn't work hard. We didn't give enough attention to restructuring that department to make it more responsive to the needs of contractors and residents, alike.

6. I was too strident in my relations with the Ramsey Board of Education, especially in the beginning of my term when I went on a crusade to try to save the old Dater School building—not for any personal aggrandizement but because I honestly felt it was a safe and less expensive alternative. I still believe that. At the time, I could have made my views known in a less confrontational way. I will not accept the view of some detractors that the mayor should keep silent on school issues. When schools represent 67% of my constituents' property tax bills, I claim the right, not just as a citizen but as a community leader, to speak out. And that includes speaking out against the rising costs of teacher benefits, pay increases, and pensions. When seniors living on fixed incomes are forced to sell homes they have lived in for 40 or 50 years and raised their children in, when they must leave family, friends, doctors and other close relationships behind because they can no longer afford property taxes, when they're banished to so-called "adult-living" communities in Toms River, or points farther south, our town will become the poorer for it. I cherish having these old-timers around, listening to their stories, and having their dignity and character serving as guideposts for our young

people. God forbid we become a homogenized community of thirty-something or forty-something upwardly mobile couples with 2.3 kids.

Printed in the United States
96323LV00004B/163-180/A